PSYCHOSYNTHESIS
COUNSELLING

Second Edition

Diana Whitmore

SAGE Publications
London • Thousand Oaks • New Delhi

First edition published 1991. Reprinted 1992, 1994, 1995, 1998
Second edition first published 2000

SAGE Publications Ltd
6 Bonhill Street
London EC2A 4PU

SAGE Publications Inc
2455 Teller Road
Thousand Oaks, California 91320

SAGE Publications India Pvt Ltd
32, M-Block Market
Greater Kailash – I
New Delhi 110 048

British Library Cataloguing in Publication data

A catalogue record for this book is
available from the British Library

ISBN 0 7619 6320 0
ISBN 0 7619 6321 9 (pbk)

Library of Congress catalog record available

Typeset by M Rules
Printed in Great Britain by Biddles Ltd, Guildford, Surrey

PSYCHOSYNTHESIS
COUNSELLING IN ACTION

Series Editor: Windy Dryden

SAGE's bestselling *Counselling in Action* series has gone from strength to strength, with worldwide sales of well over 250,000 copies. Since the first volumes in the series were published, the number of counselling courses has grown enormously, resulting in continuing demand for these introductory texts.

In response, and to keep pace with current developments in theory and practice, SAGE are pleased to announce that new and expanded editions of six of the volumes have now been published.

These short, practical books – developed especially for counsellors and students of counselling – will continue to provide clear and explicit guidelines for counselling practice.

New editions in the series include:

Feminist Counselling in Action, Second Edition
Jocelyn Chaplin

Gestalt Counselling in Action, Second Edition
Petrūska Clarkson

Transcultural Counselling in Action, Second Edition
Patricia d'Ardenne and Aruna Mahtani

Rational Emotive Behavioural Counselling in Action, Second Edition
Windy Dryden

Psychodynamic Counselling in Action, Second Edition
Michael Jacobs

Person-Centred Counselling in Action, Second Edition
Dave Mearns and Brian Thorne

Personal Construct Counselling in Action, Second Edition
Fay Fransella and Peggy Dalton

Transactional Analysis Counselling in Action, Second Edition
Ian Stewart

Standards and Ethics for Counselling in Action, Second Edition
Tim Bond

CONTENTS

FOREWORD

Insight. Each move, each effort in counselling, is directed towards that moment: the face relaxes, the eyes brighten, there is a smile of recognition. As tensions and suspicions fade away, your client sees his or her personality and life from a new perspective. There is a feeling of lightness. There is, perhaps, gratitude.

Perhaps you, the counsellor, have fought a hundred battles, met countless resistances. It was hard and tiring. But all that is now past. A fresh understanding has dawned, which is just what both counsellor and client were aiming for.

What *is* insight, and how is it produced? Although many have formulated hypotheses, no one truly knows. To facilitate understanding and transformation is less a matter of technical knowledge than one of instinct and experience.

You could compare it with skiing: good skiers know in their cells how to turn with ease, how to balance their weight exactly and dance gracefully down the slopes, while Sunday skiers come tumbling painfully down, getting stuck in deep snow, making a nuisance of themselves or even being a danger to others.

The field of counselling is just like that. Some people, improvising themselves as counsellors, try to convert their clients to their own views, or unconsciously attribute to them their own problems. Seeing themselves as great rescuers, they invade their clients' lives with their own emotions, get angry at their resistances or upset by their pain, judge them harshly or push them to change, thereby confusing them even more in their predicaments. They are the Sunday skiers of the helping professions.

Others are like champion skiers: they make the right intervention at the right moment, they glide through the asperities and the dangers of the client's inner world with great ease. They evoke the best resources in their clients, and assist them in becoming what they choose to be.

Diana Whitmore definitely belongs to this second category. For many years I have worked with her in the training of psychosynthesis professionals. And many, many times I have seen her extend her intuition while working with participants. And I have seen her accompany many of them into a freedom beyond their blocks.

Don't expect to learn her art by reading this book. That cannot be communicated. But you may expect the next best thing: if you have any interest in counselling, this is a good place to start; if you are studying to be a counsellor, this book will give you a balanced view and help bring out the best in you; if you are already working in this field, you may find new vistas and surprising directions.

Psychosynthesis counselling is innovative. It is an energetic, pragmatic approach aimed at producing results easily and quickly. It emphasizes the will and the human capacity to choose; it makes ample use of imagery; it acknowledges the presence of a transpersonal realm in all human beings – the realm of inspiration, awe and joy; it encourages clients to work on their own using a variety of specific techniques.

All good counselling has stringent requirements. A good counsellor has to be clear, feel at ease with the inner world, meet serenely with pain and rage, deal with the unexpected effectively and, above all, be open and receptive to others.

And yet, beyond all the dilemmas and demands, one finds a great beauty in counselling – in all counselling. Helping people to discover themselves, make decisions and change their attitude is a creative endeavour. Again and again, you deal with life's most profound questions: Why am I here? How can I deal with pain and solitude? What is love? What course shall I give to my existence?

Psychosynthesis Counselling in Action is a powerful contribution to meeting the challenges of counselling and appreciating its beauty.

Piero Ferrucci PhD
Centro di Studi di Psicosintesi R.Assagioli
Florence

PREFACE TO THE SECOND EDITION

In the years since the first edition of this book two important things have happened within the international psychosynthesis community. It has deepened and elaborated its understanding of what we call *transpersonal psychology*, and the need of humanity for goodness and the creation of well-being has greatly increased. From our continued and worsening social problems, to the dangers of genetic engineering; from the decline of our natural resources, to the increased violations of human rights, mankind today is having to cope with an acceleration of stress. Today we are sorely in need of a more positive meaning to our lives. Amid the noise and struggle, we need to find a place within ourselves, which is untouched by the clamour, which is still and quiet and, most importantly, which can perceive our life and world in an optimistic and beneficent way. Without wanting to sound arrogant, I believe that this book is more needed today than it was when first published. The need for psychology and counselling is to see beyond the client's presenting issues and to recognize that being human is ultimately a spiritual experience and one which includes life's problems but goes so far beyond them. While this book contains much practical input on confronting one's problems from a solid psychological basis, I wholeheartedly recommend that special attention is paid to Chapters 6 and 7 which take us deeper towards the transpersonal explanation and work with those same problems.

In psychosynthesis the greater understanding of the transpersonal has enabled us to better fulfil the above need both for enrichment of psychology and for the good of those seeking counselling. We have expanded both our interpretation of and our model for an individual's psychological suffering and dis-ease. When presented with a client's problems or issues, most psychologies tend to interpret them through an explanation of past traumas or the client's historical, past experiential background. Although this level of an individual's experience is worthy of exploration, it will not bring true healing, happiness or fulfilment. James Hillman (1996) in his best-selling book, *The Soul's Code*, postulated 'the parental fallacy'. That is, to believe that an individual's challenges in life are purely the result of childhood conditioning is a fallacy. It is a shortcoming for us to assume that an individual is purely the result of nature or nurture. We can also aim for a full transpersonal explanation of an individual's suffering – that the deepest reason for our pain and suffering (whatever our issue) is that we have forgotten who we really are. The true source of our suffering may lie in this 'forgetting', the betrayal, the loss of contact with our essential nature or Self and the meaningful journey life is meant to be for each of us.

There is a growing tendency in the psychosynthesis community to reframe pathology, as being in some way intimately connected with our soul's journey through life, rather than being a distraction or obstacle. The implicit context here is that each of us is on a journey. We each have challenges to meet and obstacles to overcome in order to fulfil ourselves. It is this context which will illuminate and give meaning to our own, or to our client's personal circumstances. In this sense our psychological *symptoms* serve as a *symbol* – a symbol that constitutes a transparent statement. This symbolic statement is the very thing that is guiding us towards the healing we are seeking, not something to eliminate in order to be well.

We could call it the *principle of hidden longing*. If we feel impotent, perhaps we feel powerless to express our true self. If we are depressed, perhaps our depression is a symptom of how we have lost touch with our truest nature. If we have lost everything that is precious and most beautiful, if we have betrayed our deepest Self, of course we will feel depressed. If we have lost the richness of our Being, perhaps we seek it desperately through the acquisition of material wealth. For another example think of joy. We try to regain the joy of being alive and in touch with ourselves by doing things that give us pleasure – alcohol, drugs, compulsive working – we seek ecstasy, but a material ecstasy, an imitation.

This, of course, is not to say that we do not explore and work with childhood trauma. A psychosynthesis counselling session will look very similar to other forms of counselling such as Psychodynamic, Person Centred, or Gestalt. Perhaps the pain of the traumas we have lived through also emphasizes the deeper pain of having given up the freedom, order and beauty that we once had – of having lost something most precious, of not being in touch with our Self. All counselling ultimately is to achieve the recovery of the Self, our Self. Dis-ease comes from a denial of the Self.

Today psychosynthesis theorists and practitioners speak of the principle of *transcendence/immanence*. Through the process of counselling there will be moments when the client re-discovers or re-connects with their true Self, moments of transcending the everyday reality and reaching a wider, higher perspective on our difficulties. We may experience a sense of the fundamental alrightness of our life, in spite of and with, the issues that we are struggling to overcome. At other moments of counselling we might see our Self deeply inherent within the very problems we are seeking to solve. Both levels of embracing our journey can be healing and transformative. Every moment of our process contains within it the opportunity for growth. In this sense there is no place to get to – no end result of permanent psychospiritual health – only the journey and the full investment of ourselves in that journey. We are both Being and Becoming in the same breath.

Finally, the therapeutic relationship can be seen as the central essential factor which can, unexpectedly, restore our connection to our own Being. It is the experience of our 'I' or sense of identity that gives us the experience of being deeply connected with ourselves, *at home* with who we are, of our true individuality. It is this 'I' that connects our everyday experience with our sense of Being or personal Selfhood. This I – Self connection is what gives us a sense of continuity and provides us with an inner empathy, an intra-psychic empathic connection.

Often, those who seek counselling have lost this connection with their deeper Self, this inner empathy. The psychosynthesis counsellor will intend to *mirror* or *reflect* for the client, through their interpersonal relationship, empathic understanding and acceptance. This in turn provides a model for the client which can be internalized – a model that fully demonstrates that no matter what her issues, problems and pathologies might be, she is at core, a valuable and worthwhile individual. The client is unquestionably more than her difficulties and issues. The counselling relationship provides a *container* which holds an acceptance of both the dark and the light within the client through which she can find continuity of Being.

PREFACE TO THE FIRST EDITION

Because psychosynthesis is really a broad vision and context of personal, interpersonal, social, global and universal evolution, it is hard to define it as a form of counselling. When addressing the human soul it is, to say the least, awesome to speak of strategies and their application. There can be no therapeutic brilliance or step-by-step sequence that adequately describes the journey to Selfhood which psychosynthesis seeks to foster in clients. This for me has been the challenge of this book.

In psychosynthesis there is no 'chart on the wall' which tells the counsellor what a Self-realized human being *should* be like. There are no ultimate Truths, no recipes to follow, only the incredible wisdom of the unfolding Self and its aspiration for meaning and purpose. In the East the concept of 'dharma' promises an ideal life pattern for each individual. So too, psychosynthesis counselling has its dharma for each client which is poignantly unique.

Although psychosynthesis as a therapy has tremendous resources of principles, models and techniques at its disposal, it does not seek to *explain away* the mystery of life and human development. It values times of darkness as much as periods of joy; it encourages us to embrace the unknown with no guarantees of security; it respects the creativity of confusion, rather than ready-made certainty; and most importantly it welcomes the unexpected which shatters our attachments and fixed models. Roberto Assagioli, the founder of psychosynthesis, said, 'our working hypothesis is that evolution is a "reasonable bet"'. He challenged his students to dare to make this bet and rigorously test its validity. In eighteen years of practising psychosynthesis I have again and again been inspired by the capacity of the human spirit for self-healing and regeneration. The *bet* is worth making.

This book has to be dedicated to those others who dare to make the *bet*, both clients and counsellors, who reach out for a more fulfilling life and profession.

There are many people who contributed to the existence of this book: most importantly, my husband who attempted to transform my 'American-speak' into English idiom, and stood beside me in my moments of despair; Hetty Einzig who did the same, and prepared Nancy's case history; all the staff of the Psychosynthesis and Education Trust; and Piero Ferrucci, my friend and colleague, who offered advice and support. A heartfelt thanks to Judith Firman who, as my 'partner in crime' over our long years of work together, has expanded and elaborated psychosynthesis as a therapy and contributed immensely to establishing psychosynthesis counselling in England and Europe. I thank *Nancy* for allowing me to use her case and Margo Russell for supplying the case history. Rachael Clyne, Georgiana Nye and Elisabeth Chew also provided wonderful case examples. My thanks are also due to Alison Sheriffs for her invaluable help with the references. The last-minute heroines, Sascha Doenges, Jenny Truch and Kim Simpson, gave the necessary crisis support to enable me to reach the manuscript's deadline. And finally, many thanks to Windy Dryden whose editorial input continually threw me into agony and occasionally ecstasy; but greatly improved the quality of this book!

INTRODUCTION

The essence of the psychosynthesis perspective is that each of us has a purpose in life, and has challenges and obstacles to meet in order to fulfil that purpose. This purpose is analogous to a journey in that we move forward along the path of life in a unique way, and are always in the process of becoming. Each step forward contains the possibility of actualizing our potential. Along this journey we sometimes fall down, get lost or led astray, become stuck, move forward and make discoveries, or courageously travel beyond our limitations.

Psychosynthesis fully recognizes that those seeking counselling need to accept and address their destructive and negative elements and integrate their personality but it also values and actively works with the uncovering of a deeper identity, the Self – our true essence beyond all masks and conditioning. A psychosynthesis counsellor approaches the client with a belief in the client's capacity to understand life, to make choices and to transcend apparent limitations. The counsellor views the client's problems and difficulties not as the result of mere inadequacy, but rather as challenges and opportunities for growth.

A psychosynthesis counsellor will acknowledge the higher reaches of human experience and endeavour to facilitate their practical realization in the client's everyday life while remaining sensitive to the depth of her suffering and the impact of childhood history on adult behaviour. Psychosynthesis respects the profundity, wisdom and power of the unconscious and offers principles and methods for co-operating with the psyche's inherent thrust towards mature self-realization. It focuses on the interdependency between personal experience and development, and the potential for creative living. Values, meaning, peak experience and the unquantifiable, ineffable essence of human life are recognized as integral elements in the counselling process.

There can be little disagreement that the counsellor or trainee counsellor today, through his or her choice of profession, is facing an extraordinary challenge. An abundance of people need help: some willingly seek counselling, others choose it as a last resort through an inability to cope with life, some are reluctant victims of psychosomatic illness and many are suffering major life crises. People are increasingly feeling ill-equipped to deal with domestic, social and even international crises. They are confronted with problems from family conflicts and divorce, and the subtle breaking down of the nuclear family. Unhealthy social relationships, unemployment, economic and environmental stress all play their part, as do less attributable feelings of anxiety, aggression, impotence, despair and meaninglessness.

Also among those who seek counselling are many who are basically healthy and able to function well, but who experience a sense of dissatisfaction with the quality of life and long for greater fulfilment and purpose. The choice to enter counselling reflects a life-affirming impulse which transcends the confines of conventional life. A search for meaning and a deeper identity leads to this choice. Counselling is therefore losing the stigma of implied psychological illness which in turn is resulting in people being less inhibited about undertaking psychological work.

Whatever their motivation, conscious or unconscious, people choose counselling because they want to become healthy and fulfilled. Human beings seem to possess an underlying sense of their potential which beckons them towards health and well-being, a primary need to take responsibility for their life and to experience it as valuable. These are potent motivating forces, which can expand the context of counselling and add a positive framework. Psychosynthesis counselling holds these principles as fundamental and seeks to evoke conscious awareness of them.

A major challenge which every caring counsellor faces is working with the pain and pathology of his or her clients while maintaining a holistic and positive perception of that person. Psychosynthesis counselling is based on a vision of human life which confronts pain and neuroses but within the wider context of evoking and strengthening that which is good, right and beautiful.

This book is for counselling practitioners, counsellors in training and for potential clients interested in this form of counselling. The book's purposes are those of:

- introducing the reader to the vision, principles and primary techniques of psychosynthesis;
- demonstrating the practice of psychosynthesis in counselling with case examples and an in-depth case history;
- enlarging the context of counselling to include that which is beyond pathology: the creative potential and possibility for meaning in the lives of those seeking it;
- expanding the field of counselling beyond the confines of symptom alleviation and problem-solving;
- demonstrating that evolution is a *reasonable hypothesis* and that there is a higher organizing principle or wisdom at work in each individual;
- nourishing tired professionals and creating a life-affirming context from which to work;
- most importantly, providing an opportunity for counsellors to work more creatively with the redemption of pain and the evocation of potential.

Rather than being a closed system, psychosynthesis offers the opportunity for immense diversity. Roberto Assagioli, its founder, purposely refrained from handing down a finished product to his students. He created its basic vision and principles while encouraging practitioners to explore and devise a large number of avenues and methods, and to integrate his empirical model with traditional psychology.

Psychosynthesis has therefore been expanded and elaborated over the years while Assagioli's basic framework determines its content and parameters. For this reason many of the models and methods have been employed in the international psychosynthesis community for years while their source often remains obscure. Suffice it to say that the content of this book, its theories and practice, belong to all psychosynthesis practitioners.

As psychosynthesis has become more well known in the helping professions, a slight distortion may have arisen. Given its inclusive nature and multitude of techniques, psychosynthesis could be mistakenly seen as an eclectic body of ideas and methods. Because the context of any psychology remains implicit except to those who have studied it in depth, it is easy to miss the substantial theoretical framework which forms the operating principles and practice of psychosynthesis.

No one model or technique is appropriate for every client all of the time. For some, dialogue is most effective, while for others a more actively dynamic mode works best. For example, the depth and subtlety of working with the unconscious using the technique of mental imagery facilitates some clients well but not others. With its wide array of techniques, psychosynthesis provides the practitioner with flexibility and variety while maintaining structural coherency.

THE USE OF GENDER

Psychosynthesis views each client, and indeed counsellor, above all as a Self, and respects the deepest essence of being human. Everyone has a Self; in fact, *is* a Self – a Being who transcends gender. We need only reflect on the most meaningful moments of our lives, when we experienced our deepest sense of self, to know the universality of Being and the redundance of gender. Of course physically and psychologically we identify ourselves as male or female, although it must be remembered that each individual contains qualities of both and some of us would benefit from some evocation of our opposite, which is often unconscious.

Throughout this book, I most often use the gender she. I do this, first, because I am a female counsellor, as are a large proportion of counsellors, and second, because the case history client is female.

1

THE PSYCHOSYNTHESIS APPROACH

Roberto Assagioli was the founding father of psychosynthesis. What led him to develop psychosynthesis? What was his background? What kind of person was he?

- As a young medical student in 1910, with much enthusiasm he introduced Sigmund Freud's psychoanalysis to his professors in Florence, and then later that year severely criticized it.
- In 1927 he proposed that the purpose of psychological healing was to contact a deeper centre of identity, the Self, to nurture its unfoldment while removing obstacles to its actualization.
- He created an optimistic vision of human nature in spite of the dominance of the pathologically orientated psychology of that time; and maintained this vision for sixty years.
- He dared to emphasize the Soul, man's spiritual Being, by postulating that this was the source of psychological health.
- He recognized the need for meaning and purpose as being fundamental to human existence and well-being.
- He perceived life as an evolutionary journey of development and differentiation, and problems as opportunities which aid this unfoldment.
- He viewed a human being as both individual with unique qualities, and as universal, intimately interconnected both with others and with the environment.

- He maintained that the active evocation of potential was necessary for the treatment of neurosis and pathology.
- He noticed that people not only repress the unacceptable aspects of themselves but also their higher impulses such as intuition, altruism, creative inspiration, love and joy.

It is useful to place Assagioli in his historical context. As a young medical doctor he was in his prime at the time when Einstein was developing his theory of relativity in Berne, Freud was pioneering psychoanalysis in Vienna, James Joyce was revolutionizing literature in Trieste, Jung was giving birth to analytical psychology in Zurich, Lenin was formulating the Russian revolution in Zurich and Heidegger was preparing to espouse existentialism in Fribourg. Most of the great intellectual revolutions were initiated in central Europe around this time, and everywhere new trends of thought were springing up.

In addition to his Western medical and psychoanalytic training, Assagioli studied the major world religions and was touched especially by the Hindu, Buddhist and Christian traditions. He was a friend of Martin Buber and was knowledgeable in Judaism. He practised Hatha and Raja yoga, the yoga of the body and of the mind. He was influenced by many Eastern and Western visionary approaches and was actively involved in the explosion of new thinking in the first thirty years of the nineteenth century.

In 1910, while still in his early twenties, Doctor Roberto Assagioli was the first psychoanalyst to start practising in Italy. During this period he visited Zurich to train in psychiatry with Bleuler, the pioneer who defined 'schizophrenia' and one of the first doctors to accept psychoanalysis. There he met Jung with whom he established a life-long friendship.

An abundance of contacts and interchanges was significant in Assagioli's background. Among these were: Russian esotericist P.D. Ouspensky, German philosopher Hermann Keyserling, Indian poet Rabindranath Tagore, Sufi mystic Inhayat Khan, Zen scholar D.T. Suzuki, psychologists Viktor Frankl, the founder of Logotherapy, and Robert Desoille, creator of the guided day-dream. These contacts, made before and after his separation from psychoanalysis, both inspired and motivated his creation of a wide perspective and vision, which he called psychosynthesis.

Although he was touched deeply by his studies with Freud and his exploration of the unconscious psyche, Assagioli quickly became dissatisfied and was inspired to delve into the further reaches of human nature. Thirty years later his ideas were in agreement with psychologist Abraham

Maslow who maintained that one could not draw universal conclusions or theories about human nature by extrapolating from the pathology of human beings or studying the sick psyche, but that one should study human kind in its greatest, most beautiful manifestations.

Although its roots are in psychoanalysis, psychosynthesis went beyond the two previously recognized forces in psychology, behaviourism and psychoanalysis. Freud's theory of the unconscious psyche stressed the impact and the consequence of childhood experience upon adult behaviour. Behaviourism addresses itself to dysfunctional behaviours and is used to replace them with socially acceptable and less painful adaptations. However, in the late 1950s a radical shift occurred in the field of psychology, a shift which even today is not fully integrated into conventional psychology – the emergence of the third and fourth forces, of humanistic and of transpersonal psychology.

Humanistic psychology promoted a movement away from the earlier tendency of psychology to limit itself to pathology, towards what the human being is capable of *becoming*. It studied self-actualized people and psychological health, and formulated a model of a healthy, fully functioning human being. It focused on the evocation of potential, on higher values, and on the enhancement of that which is beautiful and inherently positive in man. Psychosynthesis, which had held a similar perspective since 1910, gained more acceptance with this larger development.

Vaughan (1985: 102) tells us:

> The medical model of psychiatry provides relief for certain biologically-based conditions of mental illness, and behavioural psychology has developed a remarkable technology for the measurement, control and prediction of behaviour. Humanistic psychology provides an impressive array of techniques for emotional development, and cognitive psychology addresses the mental level par excellence. Existential psychotherapy deals with the problems of separate isolated existence, but the spiritual dimension of human experience has been largely ignored by traditional psychology and psychiatry.

Born in the late 1960s transpersonal psychology, the fourth force, took psychology one developmental step further. It enlarged the vision of health to include the search for meaning and purpose and extended the domain of psychological enquiry to include the individual's experience and aspiration for transcendence as well as the healing potential of self-transcendence. Andras Angyal, for example, addressed not only the individual's need to become autonomous, but also his need for the experience of *homonomy*, of union with the greater whole.

Transpersonal psychology recognized that the integrated personality would not only have a balanced development of the psychological functions, but also an experience of human interconnectedness and an awareness of those social conditions most conducive to fostering potential. This further development emphasized more than the power of the individual for self-regulation and responsibility. It also emphasized the creative capacity for global thinking and vision and is concerned with meta-needs, ultimate values and mystical experience. As this new field has evolved it has increasingly stressed the actualizing dimension of transpersonal experience.

Psychosynthesis, as one of the prime forces in transpersonal psychology, stretches beyond the boundaries of personal psychology and individuality by postulating a deeper centre of identity: the Self, our essential Being. It includes, but transcends, our personal day-to-day consciousness, leading to an enhanced sense of life direction and purpose. It is the postulate of the *Self*, the value placed upon exploration of creative potential, and the hypothesis that each individual has a purpose in life that primarily differentiates transpersonal from humanistic psychology. At the transpersonal level we find many important aspects of being human; acts of altruism, creative and artistic inspiration, the perception of beauty, intuition, curiosity about the universe and our place in it, and a sense of the universality of life.

We can perceive these four forces of psychology as a developmental flow with each force representing a step forward and a transcendence of what has come before. Viewed in isolation they form unique psychologies, each with their own contribution and therapeutic system. If framed as an evolutionary unfoldment, each force builds upon the strengths and includes the best of what existed previously. Psychosynthesis seeks to incorporate elements of each of these forces in psychology while further stepping into the exploration of values, meaning, peak experience and the ineffable essence of human life.

GOALS OF PSYCHOSYNTHESIS COUNSELLING

Assagioli recognized and developed two mutually dependent aspects of psychosynthesis: *personal psychosynthesis*, which aims to foster the development of a well-integrated personality; and *transpersonal psychosynthesis*, which offers the possibility of realizing one's higher nature and purpose in life. He recognized the individual's need for meaning, both the meaning of our own individual existence and the meaning of the world in which we live, indeed of life itself.

Traditionally, psychological growth and the spiritual quest have been labelled as separate and essentially antagonistic directions. Freud and Western psychology rationalized spiritual pursuits as escapist or delusional and tended to view man's higher values and achievements as adaptations of lower instincts and drives. On the other hand, those following spiritual disciplines have often dismissed psychology as an unnecessary distraction to the path of inner awakening. Psychosynthesis seeks to integrate these interdependent levels and asserts them as complementary aspects necessary for the resolution of psychological problems and the awakening of the Self.

Although Assagioli was perhaps the first to make the above assertion, his work corresponded with Maslow's later work, 'Theory Z' (1971), where he discriminated between two types of self-actualizing people: those who were clearly healthy, free from basic deficiency needs and effectively functioning in the world; and those who achieved the above but went further in their development by recognizing the limitations of personal identity and transcending them to move towards the realization of higher values.

Personal psychosynthesis fits within the domain of humanistic psychology. It employs many techniques to assist the integration of the personality while dealing with personality deficiencies, psychological conflicts, archaic behaviour patterns and neurotic complexes. The client's ability to function effectively and invest herself fully in the achievement of a rewarding and productive life is of key importance. Hopefully, the outcome of this work is a strong sense of personal identity.

Hence the goals of psychosynthesis parallel those of humanistic psychology and in particular Maslow's concept of self-actualization. Of course the primary and most immediate objective of psychosynthesis is to alleviate suffering. Other objectives are: to evoke strengths and latent potential, to foster integration between the inner and outer world of the client, to help the client create her own life and to express herself meaningfully, to enhance the quality of life and finally to evoke the client's inner authority and wisdom thereby rendering the counsellor obsolete.

All of the above are worthy goals for counselling. To become a strong individual fully invested in life, and to function well and effectively, can be a great achievement. But what next? What is this Self? What follows when a person has attained a reasonable measure of competence and well-being? What are we to do with this hard-won psychological integration? What are the deeper values to live for? Am I evolving in a positive direction? These questions are well worth asking anyway, but the success of counselling may depend upon their exploration.

Assagioli maintained that the purpose of psychosynthesis is to help integrate, to *synthesize*, the multiple aspects of the individual's personality around a personal centre and later to effect a greater synthesis between the personal ego and the transpersonal Self. According to Kaufman (1984) Jung also postulated a similar drive towards individuation or intrinsic wholeness and believed that this force autonomously pushes us towards fulfilling our truest self. This groundwork is also essential to authentic transpersonal awakening in order to ensure that a pathology of the sublime does not replace previously neurotic symptoms.

As previously mentioned, the transpersonal dimension is that area of the human psyche which is qualitatively higher than, and which transcends, personal existence. It is the home of greater aspirations, the source of higher feelings like compassion and altruism, and forms the roots of intuition and creative intelligence. Transpersonal awareness emerges in different ways at different times. At any point in adult life an individual may experience an inner awakening, a longing for life to be more deeply fulfilling and inspiring than it previously has been. This awakening is not necessarily religious by nature.

There can be an inflow of superconscious energies, peak experiences in Maslow's terms, which momentarily foster clarity of vision, a transcendence of personal identity, an awareness of the oneness of all life, and may provide experiences of a qualitative nature like serenity, love and beauty. Transpersonal experiences have a reality which many feel to be more profound than normal everyday existence. They embody an intrinsic value, a noetic quality, leaving the individual with a deepened sense of value and meaning.

It is also not unusual for transpersonal interests to be evoked by a trauma or serious disruption in a person's life. A divorce, an accident, a near-death experience can force an individual to let go of something to which she was attached and in which she had invested a great deal of life energy. This disruption can lead to questioning the significance of life and a search for meaning and answers beyond individuality.

LEVELS OF PSYCHOSYNTHESIS COUNSELLING

The purpose of this section is to establish the groundwork of psychosynthesis counselling by examining the three psychological levels which it addresses: the past, the present and the future. At the heart of psychosynthesis is its emphasis on the *transpersonal*, the primary factor differentiating it from other schools of counselling. This section also includes an introduction to the transpersonal dimension.

The Past

Freud's work demonstrated that various physical symptoms and psychological disturbances were due to instincts, drives and fantasies buried in the unconscious and retained there by resistances and defence mechanisms. It is an exaggeration to say that we are our history and yet it is commonly understood that our past and childhood experiences influence how we behave as adults. This influence is multi-dimensional, often indirect and pervasive. It profoundly affects our capacity for love and intimacy, for assertion and self-affirmation; it determines our perception of life, and colours our deepest attitudes and values. Unless we are to remain puppets of the past, our neurotic elements must be brought into consciousness and transformed.

Assagioli (1965: 21) believed that the first step towards self-actualization was a thorough knowledge of one's personality. He wrote:

> We have to recognize that in order to really know ourselves, it is not
> enough to make an inventory of the elements that form our conscious
> being. An extensive exploration of the vast regions of our unconscious
> must also be undertaken. We first have to penetrate courageously into
> the pit of our lower unconscious in order to discover dark forces that
> ensnare and menace us – the phantasms, the ancestral or childish
> images that obsess or silently dominate us, the fears that paralyze us,
> the conflicts that waste our energies.

In this sense the counsellor must begin by assessing the personality's blocks and potentials to allow a purposeful exploration of the underworld of the unconscious. In order to reach the roots of psychological complexes, childhood experiences are uncovered with particular regard to the impact they currently have on the client's life.

The lower unconscious in psychosynthesis corresponds to the *unconscious* in traditional psychology. This contains:

1 the elementary psychological activities which direct the life of the body; the intelligent co-ordination of bodily functions;
2 the fundamental drives and primitive urges;
3 many complexes charged with intense emotions;
4 various pathological manifestations, such as phobias, obsessions, compulsive urges and paranoid delusions;
5 a reservoir of childhood experiences, stored as memories, some of which may have a traumatic nature.

Few of us had a childhood free from negative conditioning and the limitations of our parents. We may have experienced a sense of betrayal by the adults upon whom we were so dependent and to whom so vulnerable. Nearly all of us retain 'unfinished business' with our parents; pain and psychological dysfunction may lie in a client's original relationships with mother, father or primary caretakers. It is not that all parents are bad. Perhaps they were not psychologically mature enough to parent well or they themselves lacked positive models. As children we sometimes fall prey to the unfulfilled needs and expectations of our parents, and to conditional loving.

In addition to the problems which stem from parental relationships, the conditioning that we receive from our culture may later create difficulties. Childhood experiences are stored in the lower unconscious, and have an effect on the development of our personality which in turn penetrates our future behaviour. A therapeutic relationship can provide a safe, inclusive environment for a person to re-experience painful feelings that were repressed in the past, which experience liberates their controlling influence.

Negative childhood experiences do not sit quietly in the basement of our psyche. Repression, suppression or denial of feelings creates emotional stress. The unconscious is not a bin of static past experience but rather a dynamic process of psychological activities of which we are unaware. Every psychological problem has its own historical background which often remains unconscious and distorts behaviour. The psychosynthesis counsellor works extensively to help the client release the grip of the past and learn to express real but buried feelings in the present. When a natural capacity for expression of feelings is redeemed, emotional health can be reestablished.

Perception is also conditioned and coloured by past experiences. From these experiences, defence mechanisms are formed, which preserve the stability of the personality but do so at the expense of distorting reality. They lower anxiety in order to maintain a stable level of functioning. So initially these defences serve the person well but later they restrict growth. Ghosts from the past must be liberated and repressed psychological energy freed if their destructive impact on adult life is not to lead to pain and restricted functioning.

Psychosynthesis contends that the past may have an even deeper function in determining the *quality* of adult life. A person's inner life may be incongruent with their outer life, contributing to a sense of inauthenticity. As a result the integrity of feeling at home in the world may be lacking. On a mental level, too, our history influences our attitudes, beliefs and philosophies about life, which further affects the quality of our life today. We may for example believe that: 'People cannot be trusted'; 'I have to fight for what I want'; 'Life is all pain and suffering'. These basic but often unconscious attitudes condition our image of reality.

To consciously and deeply understand our psychological history can liberate a sense of meaning – of life being more than merely a disordered existence. Although neurotic behaviour patterns which are not of our own making manifest in all of us, they need not be permanent, inevitable or irrevocable. It is within our capacity to change them.

The Present

Assagioli considered it wise for counselling work to move from the known to the unknown. The counsellor will start with an inventory and assessment of known components of the personality, not in a vague and passive way, but with conscious understanding. The stronger the personality, the more readily are unconscious elements assimilated and the more fruitful a redemption of the past will be.

Those seeking counselling do so because they find difficulty in their present everyday lives which causes them stress and inhibits their functioning. They have *symptoms*, behaviour patterns and ways of relating which are distorted and restrictive. A psychosynthesis counsellor will help the client to formulate, clarify and define the issues that are troubling her.

In psychosynthesis counselling the *presenting issue* is not taken simply at face value. The counsellor will intend to explore the breadth and depth of its impact on the client's current life in the following areas:

- the manifestations of the presenting issue in the client's life;
- the situations which evoke the problem: when and how they do this;
- the interpersonal relationships involved and the roles they play in the client's life;
- the physical sensations accompanying the presenting issue;
- the predominant emotions that are involved;
- the beliefs, attitudes and opinions that it stimulates.

The counsellor frames areas of pain and difficulty as *signals* that the client is not heading in the right direction and *pointers* to the way forward. Problems are not simply pathological states to be eliminated but rather indicators of a hidden thrust towards integration. When the counsellor collaborates with the inevitable by perceiving the presenting issue as a progressive way forward, this revolutionizes the context of counselling. By confronting pathology with this attitude, the client can discover a more meaningful context for living. Paradoxically, in facing death, depression, anxiety and pain the client may discover meaning and a deeper identity.

In Assagioli's differentiation of the unconscious the present corresponds to the 'middle unconscious', which is formed of psychological elements similar to our waking consciousness, containing the memories, thoughts and feelings of which our everyday life is woven. This awareness is readily accessible to us merely by choosing to remember. The middle unconscious contains recent or near-present experiences or occurrences. It points not to what we have been or to what we could be, but to the evolutionary state we have actually reached. Assagioli notes that in this region our various experiences are assimilated with the ordinary mental and imaginative activities which are being elaborated and developed in a sort of psychological gestation, immediately before their birth into the light of consciousness.

The Future

Obstacles may point towards the recognition of a limited identity which the client is unconsciously ready to shed. As a snake sheds its skin, the client outgrows the old behaviour patterns contained within a problem. She will experience pain and the need for change in precisely those areas where a new identity is trying to emerge – the next level of integration. The more the counsellor and client consciously collaborate, the greater the progress possible. Alternatively, if the client blindly repeats old patterns, increased pain and crystallization will result. Much suffering is generated through the perpetuation of old identities and resistance to change.

In psychosynthesis counselling, the future is seen as the realm of potential – what we may be, and indeed what we are becoming. Our potential
symbolizes the next evolutionary step forward, not yet actualized. It contains our hidden resources, our latent possibilities for creativity and our
positive strengths and qualities. In psychosynthesis the 'superconscious' is
a level of the unconscious which is qualitatively higher than the lower
unconscious in an evolutionary rather than a moral sense. This 'higher
unconscious' is the home of our greater aspirations, intuitions and
transpersonal energies. It is the seat of artistic, philosophical, scientific
and ethical revelations and impulses to humanitarian action. Assagioli
described this realm as the source of higher feelings such as altruistic
love, of creative intelligence and of states of contemplation, illumination
and ecstasy. The superconscious also functions as a higher organizing
principle which oversees the evolution of the individual.

On occasion most of us have had a superconscious experience, of varying degrees of intensity, when for a moment we touched our essential
nature, or our true Self. Maslow (1954: 164) defined such superconscious
experiences as 'peak experiences', in which

> there were feelings of limitless horizons opening up to the vision, the
> feeling of being simultaneously more powerful and also more helpless
> than one ever was before, the feeling of great ecstasy and wonder and
> awe, the loss of placing in time and space, with finally, the conviction
> that something extremely important and valuable had happened, so
> that the subject is to some extent transformed and strengthened even in
> his daily life by such experiences.

Peak experiences are accorded much value in psychosynthesis and are
framed as intimately connected with the client's daily life and presenting
problems. What this means for counselling practice is that each presenting
issue contains a creative possibility and an opportunity for growth. Some
potential is seeking to be born; something developmentally more
advanced is trying to emerge for the client.

This idea implies that problems and obstacles at their deepest level are
inherently meaningful, evolutionary, coherent and potentially transformative. The counsellor will recognize that it is no accident that various
conflicts become foreground issues at particular times. Old psychological
forms die (the past) in order for new ones to be born (the future). The
energy of conflict is the energy of transformation. Working with potential

in the process of change involves the counsellor having the capacity to perceive what is trying to be born *through* the difficulty, and that she value creative dissonance.

THE TRANSPERSONAL DIMENSION IN PSYCHOSYNTHESIS COUNSELLING

The Search for Unity

The transpersonal dimension of psychosynthesis speaks to a human longing which seems to be universal – a deep yearning for the experience of unity. Unity with ourselves: self-respect, the experience of being a worthwhile human being, is central to that yearning. Unity with others: the urge to love and be loved motivates much of our behaviour although it is often unconscious and distorted. Unity with society: it can be said that it is the lack of this which is at the core of fear and hostility. Without the experience of unity, life is liable to become increasingly fragmented and meaningless.

This yearning for unity can underlie many symptoms: a chronic feeling of isolation; self-destructive behaviour such as alcohol or drug consumption which dulls reality and creates a false sense of unity; suicidal impulses which may suggest an unconscious desire to return to security and the *primal* unity of the womb; existential despair and hopelessness; dissatisfaction with a long-hoped-for successful career. These are just a few of many similar examples taken from my experience as a counsellor.

The Experience of Rightness

Transpersonal psychosynthesis responds to an individual's search for *rightness*, the desire to know who we are and where we are going. All too often outer authorities are sought for answers to inner questions, yet we may experience a pervasive need to come *home* to ourselves, to find a resting place within. Through transpersonal work the client may find her inner authority which has surprisingly little to do with outer validation. This inner authority implies certainty and is deeply connected with a sense of self.

Along this line, clients have discovered the ability to *know* what is best for them, what their next step in life is, and how to heal and direct their own development. For example, a client who has been told repeatedly that her experienced reality is not valid will develop a poor self-image and mistrust her own perception. The experience of *rightness* leads to a shift from environmental support to self-support. Increasingly the client may feel free to make choices that appear irrational or *not like her* but reflect enhanced self-direction. Examples of this would be a change of career at the peak of a hard-won success, a simplification of life-style, a rejection of previously held values, or an altruistic action which is uncomfortable.

It is not uncommon for a client to present feelings of despair and imprisonment. She is often unconsciously striving to make sense of her life and to order it into a meaningful pattern, one which potentially includes both her joy and sorrow, her fears and her dreams. The distressing content of a person's life (ageing, the death of a loved one, the loss of a cherished job) may not necessarily be changed by counselling, but *how* that content is perceived and valued and the place it occupies in the person's thoughts may undergo surprising alterations. As Aldous Huxley is remembered for saying, 'Experience is not what happens to a man. It is what a man does with what happens to him.' An expanded, enriched sense of meaning often accompanies an exploration and subsequent awakening of the transpersonal dimension.

Social Value

Working on a transpersonal level has social value in that many clients who explore it discover a sense of interconnectedness. They begin to choose, both in thought and action, interdependence over independence and autonomy. An awareness of universality and of belonging to the larger whole of life carries deep implications for one's role in society. Our ability to discriminate between means and ends is enhanced. It is not just *what* one does that matters, but *how* one does it. Life itself becomes the arena for creative self-expression, which is often contributory. It is not unusual in psychosynthesis counselling, for example, for the client to re-evaluate her choice of career, or the implications of her actions upon other people, or the goals which she previously cherished.

The Self

Working transpersonally goes beyond the boundaries of a client's individuality. It is hard to define the transpersonal Self because it cannot be easily expressed in words or abstract concepts. It is a living experience for which we find metaphors in all cultures: Ulysses' *Odyssey* – a long journey whose purpose is to find a way home; Dante's *Divine Comedy* in which Dante eventually reaches heaven, but only after he experiences hell, purgatory and confronts his shadow; the Holy Grail, for which man searches to find the source of life and immortality. There are many stories and many versions of each, yet they have a single common theme: that there is a centre of life, a place where we feel whole and complete, and that this lies within ourselves. The source of being within, or Self, is not a passive presence, but capable of a profound and meaningful empathic relationship with an individual's everyday experience of life. The deeper will of the Self is felt as an invitation to a purposeful existence. The realization of this source is the heart of transpersonal work. Assagioli maintained that the ultimate purpose of psychosynthesis is to help release the experience of the Self and to recognize it as the organizing principle of life.

Conventional psychology does not acknowledge this centre of life, known in psychosynthesis as the transpersonal or spiritual Self. Humanistic psychologists, however, have sought to include it. Carl Rogers claimed to work with the organismic self; Fritz Perls termed it the 'point of creative indifference' and spoke of organismic self-regulation; Abraham Maslow stressed the need in all human beings for self-actualization; James Bugental encouraged a search for the lost sense of Being. Both Carl G. Jung and Roberto Assagioli, the fathers of transpersonal psychology, dedicated their work to bringing this *soul* into the foreground of modern psychology.

The Self can be described as a person's most authentic identity, the deepest experience of Being. It can be a conscious experience for some, while for others it may be latent until superconscious experiences stimulate awareness of its existence. Experiences of beauty, of creative intelligence, of illumination, of insight into the purpose of life, and of altruistic imperatives can awaken the individual to this deeper identity.

For one client, moments of oneness with the beauty of nature stimulated its awakening. Another found that the creative experience of childbirth, both for herself and others present, led to an awareness of the transpersonal dimension. Inspired scientists have found transcendence through scientific discovery. One client who did volunteer work with the elderly experienced fulfilment through helping others, which evoked for her a sense of solidarity.

It is worth noting that the awakening of the Self may also be stimulated by crisis and negative experiences. For one client, the death of a loved one stimulated a search for meaning which led her to the experience of the Self; another, overwhelmed by a mid-life crisis, found relief through deep acceptance of her being which altered her priorities and life direction. For an overstressed businessman, the loss of his valued career shocked him into a transcendent experience of his true identity far beyond his role as a businessman. These insights are often gained through the work of transpersonal counselling. In times of stress, many in psychosynthesis counselling have experienced a movement towards a wider perspective and a greater sense of proportion.

In this sense there is nothing esoteric about the Self or the transpersonal domain. It is a familiar and intimate experience, but one which we must discover for ourselves. Life itself is the journey through which we discover and realize our being. It is long and often arduous, and includes all manner of experience, dark moments as well as periods of light. It contains outer as well as inner experience, and offers no short cuts and no easy answers. It is the journey T.S. Eliot speaks of in his *Four Quartets:*

> We shall not cease from exploration
> And the end of all our exploring
> Will be to arrive where we started
> And know the place for the first time.

No Guarantees

Transcendent states of consciousness are not by themselves a guarantee of effective psychological functioning, and when improperly handled can cause a wide variety of psychological problems. If the personality is not stable and integrated, superconscious experience can lead to mental imbalance. Those who are immature may escape into the transpersonal domain as an unconscious way of avoiding the difficulties of life. The personal ego may become inflated by glimpses of the essential Self and the divinity of life. An inner awakening can evoke an enhanced vision of potential so immense that it leads to chronic dissatisfaction with reality. In effect the transpersonal, if misused or misunderstood, can multiply neuroses.

For these important reasons psychosynthesis attempts to integrate the personal with the transpersonal and to facilitate the client's healthy expression of these psychospiritual energies. Addressing the transpersonal domain in psychosynthesis counselling is not a mystical avoidance of reality, nor does it promote transcendence of, or withdrawal from, everyday life. It aims to clear the way for and encourage transpersonal experience, to enable a person to use their resources in an ordered way for growth. A rich spiritual life, peak experiences, an honest vision of one's potential and a sense of unity may lead only to despair unless the client is capable of translating them into everyday life. Hence, at the core of psychosynthesis counselling is both the *experience* and the *expression* of the transpersonal dimension.

Transpersonal experience emerges in different ways for different individuals, and as a consequence there is no prescribed recipe to follow. Psychosynthesis counselling is a co-operative interplay in which the course of work will be dictated by the client's motivation and unfoldment.

Having looked at the goals and levels of psychosynthesis counselling, the next chapter will explore the role of the counsellor and the counsellor as a person. Most modern theories of counselling agree that the relationship between counsellor and client is at the core of successful counselling. The counsellor's *presence* is the very heart of the training of a psychosynthesis counsellor.

2

THE PSYCHOSYNTHESIS COUNSELLOR

THE CONTEXT OF PSYCHOSYNTHESIS COUNSELLING

Caroline sat on the edge of her chair, spine erect, obviously trying to hold herself together and said in a flat, dull voice, 'I'm afraid I'm going mad. I'm depressed and can't seem to get on with living. I can't go on like this and yet I don't know what to do.' Here was a person relatively unknown to the counsellor. A new client, a new beginning; a unique human being, but with definable pain and psychological symptoms similar to ones the counsellor had met before. How does the counsellor begin to interpret and frame the process, both psychological and transpersonal, that will unfold during the counselling journey?

The relationship between the counsellor and the client is the place to begin to look at the context of psychosynthesis counselling. A psychological context is that which illuminates and gives meaning to a particular set of circumstances. It is the ground on which a counsellor's operating principles and her attitude towards the client stand. Although implicit, covert and often unconscious, this context will profoundly influence her work. Psychosynthesis assumes that something more is going on for the client than merely a problem to be solved, a crisis to be survived or pain to be alleviated.

Although it may not be made explicit as a goal of the therapeutic process, psychosynthesis counselling aims to achieve something more while working with the client's problems and predicament: the discovery and expression of an increasingly purposeful and creative life, rich with meaning and value. A counsellor must be conscious of and understand her own set of assumptions about human nature, pathology and human potential if the work is to be more than just symptom resolution. Watzlawick (1974) speaks of two kinds of change. *First-order change* is merely rearranging the content of the psyche and can end up with the solution contributing to the problem. *Second-order change* changes the total context of what is happening; it changes the system within which the problem is operating and is the only real change. In psychosynthesis the context that *illuminates and gives meaning* to the client's circumstances is one which regards the client as ultimately a Self, a Being who has a purpose in life and has challenges and obstacles to meet in order to fulfil that purpose.

Wilber (1980) has likened the counselling arena to a building in which each floor represents a different level of consciousness. Counselling can remain on one floor for a long time, incessantly moving the furniture around (the contents of the client's consciousness) or it can create a transformation by shifting to a higher level or context. Psychosynthesis maintains that the process is not a linear one, but one in which the higher level or transpersonal context is held by the counsellor while the content of the client's distress is worked through. As Caroline begins to elaborate her problems and pour out her distress, the psychosynthesis counsellor will address these very real and painful issues but at the same time will watch for and facilitate deeper questions of meaning and the potential transformation which may be emerging through them.

She will ask herself, 'What's trying to emerge through this difficulty? What's seeking expression in this person's life?' For example, Caroline's depression may be a symbol of a life bereft of fulfilling relationships, but the potential for intimacy and healthy self-affirmation may be emerging. Another client, who found herself unable to establish a long-term relationship with a man, experienced repeated anxiety attacks. During counselling she discovered an inner critic constantly undermining her attempts to relate. The experience of loving and valuing *herself* had to emerge before it would be possible for her to enter an intimate relationship.

Health is not a static condition that is achieved once and for all, but a dynamic on-going process of change. It is interwoven with all the elements of well-being, and depends on the integration of physical, emotional, mental, existential and spiritual levels of consciousness. The *contents* of our awareness and experience are constantly in a state of flux. The nature of the life process seems to be one of a continual disruption in the personality. Old forms are dying, new ones are being born. If the context that we hold causes us to work solely from the level of content, we will find that *something* is always missing, *something* is not available to us. We are aware of our lack of lovableness, or potency, or alrightness or security, and we cannot be whole without it. Our context is impoverished and counselling merely seeks to provide what is missing, rather than transform underlying growth patterns. In the absence of a consciously created context, our lives will be controlled by the content.

An alternative context is that counselling is not so concerned with solving this or that problem, but with creating the conditions in which it can be solved or transcended. The counsellor could then focus upon assisting the client to learn *how* to handle her problems as they arise. The assumption here is that given the opportunity, the wisdom of the Self will emerge as an integrating, healing force to be trusted. Through the therapeutic process there is a way to become aware of and co-operate with this wisdom. The psychosynthesis counsellor will hold the view that the client *is* a Self (the context) who *has* a personality which is not fully integrated and is experiencing pain or crisis (the content).

A psychosynthesis counsellor is committed to a particular set of assumptions which are not absolute, but nevertheless are useful as working hypotheses. A few commonly adopted contexts are:

- The client is most essentially a Self, a Being who has a purpose in life and is on a path of unfoldment which includes challenges and obstacles of a psychological nature.
- This Self is abundant and complete and is the source of healing within the client.
- The transpersonal realm which includes experience of the Self, awareness of superconscious content and the evocation of potential and meaning is a prerequisite for both psychological health and successful counselling.
- The shadow (our darker side which contains unredeemed aspects) is integral to the human condition and needs to be integrated in the client's experience of well-being.

The psychosynthesis counsellor does not hold a normative definition of a healthy and fully functioning individual. A high value is placed on inner freedom and upon the client gaining mastery over her psychological state.

The counsellor's task is to help the client enlarge her possibilities and choices. This freedom of choice will then enable the client to live as she deems meaningful and worthwhile. She will become increasingly responsible for her inner development and outer behaviour.

THE COUNSELLOR

Freud asserted that the therapist must remain anonymous, a blank screen upon which the client would displace her neurosis and bring it to the foreground. He defined this 'transference' as the client's repetition with the therapist of early relationships with parents. He claimed that transference was universal and must always be addressed. Assagioli challenged this assumption: he believed that the therapist must emerge from anonymity and become a more active and participative human being.

Jung maintained that the bond between client and counsellor is not just a professional relationship, but a much deeper state which he called 'mystical participation'. He said that the therapist must be aware of this unconscious, but profound, *underwater* bond as an element in the therapeutic relationship. Jung was also the first to hold a humanistic view of patients. He recommended seeing the client from the perspective of health rather than from the traditional medical model of illness.

Assagioli corroborated Jung's ideas and went further in saying that transference need not be universally confronted, but that it warrants addressing only when it becomes an obstacle to the counselling. Transference can remain present but will undergo changes, gradually losing its energy over time. Assagioli observed this implicit working out of transference occurring as the personal relationship between the counsellor and client became stronger. (A more complete exploration of the phenomenon of transference will follow in Chapter 5.) This is especially true when by creating an empathic holding environment for the client, the counsellor is adequately providing an external unifying centre.

The Counsellor as an External Unifying Centre

Initially there is pain, discomfort or crisis for most individuals seeking counselling. They have no internal reference point, no stable sense of identity and often feel victim to the forces of their own psyche. Like a leaf tossed by the wind, they feel no capacity for clear awareness and vision, for being the *source and sustenance* of their existence. They have no stable centre of identity, which, in psychosynthesis, is called the 'I' or personal self. Without it, we tend to experience being a *victim* to the circumstances of our life and at the mercy of forces, both internal and external over which we have no control.

It is an experience of the 'I', or sense of identity that gives us the experience of being deeply connected with ourselves, *at home* with who we are, of our true individuality. As we will see later, this 'I' is what connects our everyday experience with the transpersonal Self, and gives us the experience of personal Selfhood. In psychosynthesis we recognize this 'I'–Self connection as fundamental to psychospiritual health. The 'I'–Self connection is what gives us a sense of continuity and provides us with an *inner empathy* or an *intra-psychic empathic connection*. We might say that this experience can also give us a sense of liking or loving ourselves and of well-being – an empathic connection with ourselves.

Alternatively, a break in this 'I'–Self connection often creates an experience of worthlessness and of having no right to exist, of not being a valuable and worthwhile person in our own right. In their model of 'the primal wound', psychosynthesis theorists John Firman and Ann Gila (1997) assert that a break in the 'I'–Self connection carries with it the threat of *non-being* or *personal annihilation* which causes us to form a *survival personality* in order to mask, hide and avoid this threat and the depth of our insecurity.

What does this mean for the psychosynthesis counsellor? The empathetic connection with ourselves is first experienced through an empathic connection with our mother or other primary caregiver early in life. In terms of intra-psychic development, we relate to our early caregiver as a part of the mother/child stage of development.

Most systems of psychology recognize the vital role that *mirroring* (Winnicott, Kohut, Miller) plays in the early development of an infant. As the infant experiences herself reflected in the caregiver's eyes, attitude towards them and on-going perception, she will experience either a celebration that she exists as a uniquely individual, worthy and lovable being, or a kind of reverse non-existence through the lack of adequate mirroring. Mirroring, or an empathic connection with the caregiver can be said to be every child's birthright – to know that he or she is fundamentally worthwhile and lovable simply because he exists. It is this vital mirroring that eventually leads to a sense of personal selfhood or the violation of which can lead to psychopathology..

We experience this empathic connection through what Assagioli called an *external unifying centre*. Our early caregivers are meant to provide a *holding environment* (Winnicott, Mahler) which adequately mirrors to us the

'I'–Self connection. The counsellor will, for a time, provide this mirroring function with those clients, and they are the majority, who did not receive this empathic mirroring as young beings. The psychosynthesis counsellor will be willing to provide an *external unifying centre* for the client, until the client is able to establish an *internal unifying centre* for herself.

The psychosynthesis counsellor makes herself available as a model of the 'I' for the client. She will, through her empathic connection to the client, demonstrate that no matter what her issues, problems and pathologies might be, she is at core, a valuable and worthwhile individual. The client is essentially *more than his or her pathology*. The counsellor models for the client unconditional positive regard, an inclusive vision and an acceptance of both the dark and the light within, and provides a *holding container* through which the client can find continuity of being. The mirroring which the counsellor provides for the client forms a mutual ground of being within which the work can occur.

Assagioli (1965) believed that, for the counsellor to provide this external reference point was important and necessary for a period of the work, as a kind of indirect self-realization. If the counsellor stays conscious and the client does not lose himself in the external object of the counsellor, the client can fully realize who he is, more deeply inside, through the external centre. The counsellor becomes an indirect but true link, a point of connection between the client and his 'I'.

Regardless of technique, current research demonstrates that the quality of the human relationship has an essential influence in determining the outcome of counselling. Without adequate mirroring and an empathic containing 'holding' of the client – without a *bifocal vision* – one which sees both the light and the shadow in clients – and without a context which perceives the client as essentially more than her pathology, the counsellor reduces the effectiveness of her work. Rogers (1961), the father of person-centred counselling, contributed much towards a wider acceptance of the significance of the counsellor-client relationship. The psychoanalyst Andras Angyal (1965) noticed that his clients consistently told him that the most meaningful aspect of their counselling was the first few minutes of greeting and chat. This feedback led him to realize the importance of the relationship between client and counsellor.

Assagioli spoke of this relationship being the very heart of the therapeutic process. He believed that without authentic human relating, trust would not be established between the counsellor and client and without this essential ingredient, little growth was possible. The more psychologically disturbed the client is, the longer it takes to build this trust.

He further elaborated the dangers of both dependency and projection of the sublime without a genuine relationship. The client might remain dependent upon the authority figure of the therapist for answers to her problems and guidance towards normative psychological health. Autonomy and a healthy separation from the counsellor would become immensely difficult. Projection of the sublime occurs when the client perceives the counsellor as more intelligent, more creative, more in possession of all the positive qualities for which she yearns.

The training of a psychosynthesis counsellor focuses as much on the counsellor as a person and her *presence* with clients as it does on the models and methods of psychosynthesis. Jung's injunction, 'Learn your theories well, but put them down when faced with the miracle of a living human soul', is particularly appropriate.

The counsellor must also be familiar with the terrain of psychospiritual development, especially her own. An essential part of her training is to experience psychosynthesis at the depth, frequency and duration of intended practice. This therapy enables her to meet clients with *presence* and an intimate knowledge of the journey upon which the client is embarking. That is not to say that the counsellor knows what the client's experience is, but that she knows the journey, and is not operating from abstract theories or technical impositions. She is then able to create a subjective ambiance which will encourage the client to go to greater depths.

Clients both unconsciously and intuitively sense whether the counsellor herself has touched the deeper recesses of her own psyche. A counsellor who has merely learned her theories well will be unable to create a safe place for the client to explore previously unknown territory. Crampton (1977: 50) writes:

> The quality of the helping relationship, based on unconditional love and close attunement to the client, is the indispensable context without which techniques are mere mechanical gimmicks which will lack true healing power. The level of the guide's (counsellor's) personal integration is a crucial element which determines the amount of clarity and love he or she is able to bring to the traveller (client) on the path.

This same principle applies to the transpersonal region of human experience. A counsellor who herself suffers from repression of the sublime – the denial of what is qualitatively higher than, and transcendent of, a separate individual existence – will be inadequate to provide the psychological arena for the client to discover that which is creative, inherently positive and consciously wise. Vaughan-Clark (1977: 80) further stresses:

> The capacity of the therapist for compassion, empathy, love and acceptance is of crucial importance in determining the level of the final outcome. The client learns to respond as the therapist responds, learns to listen to him/herself as the therapist listens. The more evolved and aware and open the therapist is, the more space the client is given for growth within the therapeutic relationship. This is just another way of saying that any psychotherapy (or counselling) is only as high as the psychotherapist (counsellor).

The Counsellor's Presence

As previously mentioned, the challenge for an effective counsellor is to maintain a holistic vision of the client while addressing her pain and pathology. When the counsellor approaches the session with a limited or partial consciousness, the client will be seen as if her presenting issue were the only reality. A danger that the counsellor may encounter is that she might become identified with a limitation of her own personality, such as the psychological state that was in the foreground for her prior to the session. Typical examples of this are: her response to a previous client who was resistant and defended, or an upsetting phone call with her mother or an argument with her husband the night before. Such a list could be endless and will be familiar to any practising counsellor.

A psychosynthesis counsellor is encouraged to develop a full *presence* and to approach each client with a universal orientation and an enlarged perspective. What does this actually mean? It means that, given the importance of authenticity and the quality of the human relationship, the counsellor meets the client as a whole person; in other words having her own bodily, emotional and mental processes available. It means including the counsellor's awareness of her own Selfhood and being attuned to her own higher qualities such as clarity, openness, love and compassion. More deeply it means having a presence of spirit and recognizing that the client is inherently more than her problem.

Thus, for example, in supervision with Assagioli, when I told him that I felt impatient with a client's progress, he suggested that I meditate on 'eternity' and tune into the timeless unfoldment of human evolution. Strangely enough, doing this enabled me to approach the client with a wider and more inclusive vision which allowed me to affirm her reality, as well as see her potential to change. This is not a technique, but a holistic attitude which addresses long-term potential rather than short-term goals.

The Pygmalion Effect

The Pygmalion effect is an old and simple idea. It suggests that one's expectations of another person's behaviour can greatly affect their behaviour, even to the extent that the expectation is likely to become true. This means that one person's unfounded belief about, or image of, another tends to be realized.

The first recorded example of this is found in Greek mythology. A sculptor, Pygmalion, created an ivory statue of a beautiful maiden, and fell hopelessly in love with his statue. Her exquisite beauty touched him so deeply, symbolizing his own ideal, that he was beside himself. Venus, the goddess of love and beauty, was so moved by this that she gave the statue life in response to the sculptor's prayer.

In George Bernard Shaw's famous play *Pygmalion* the relationship between Professor Higgins and Eliza Doolittle is a complex one, not dissimilar to the relationship between counsellor and client. It demonstrates both the positive and negative effects of expectations. Eliza Doolittle was a simple peasant girl selling flowers in the street when she met Professor Higgins. In his outward role as her teacher, Higgins encouraged Eliza to learn certain language and behaviour which would show that she was well born and bred. But deep inside he expected her to behave like a girl from the street and thus it was difficult for her to do otherwise.

As Eliza Doolittle said to an admirer, 'You see, the difference between a lady and a flower girl is not how she behaves, but how she is treated. I shall always be a flower girl to Professor Higgins because he always treats me as a flower girl and always will; but I know I can become a lady to you because you always treat me like a lady, and always will' (Insel and Jacobson, 1975: ix).

The relevance of the Pygmalion effect to the counsellor–client relationship is obvious. The counsellor may outwardly encourage the client to learn new skills and deal with her problems, while deep within (perhaps unconsciously) have a negative or limited vision of the client and her potential. Avoiding the Pygmalion effect is not merely thinking well of the client or believing that she is essentially whole and complete. It requires that the counsellor know her own psyche well enough to have confronted her implicit attitudes towards human beings, her deepest feelings about pain and suffering and even her beliefs about the nature of the universe.

The German writer Goethe also stressed the importance of the Pygmalion effect. He claimed that if we treat a person as he is, we are liable to make that person worse, because we are blocking him. This is a radical way of saying that if we see our clients as their pathology and struggles, we may make them worse, or at best contribute to them staying the way they are. Goethe also said that if we treat a person as he could be, we will help him become that.

Of course this is risky, for how can the counsellor truly know what the client could be? The danger is of imposing our own vision and aspirations on to the client, or at least forcing her to endure our therapeutic recipes for psychospiritual health and well-being. It can easily become a 'chart on the wall' dogma of optimal psychological health which is blindly applied to all clients.

If the actualization of the client's potential is to be achieved, an authentic sense of meaning and purpose must come from within, rather than from an outer authority. This is more likely to happen with the inclusion of the transpersonal domain, which offers a systematic exploration of the client's positive qualities, both latent and actual, and works to uncover her deepest experience of Self. If the counsellor is familiar with the client's experience of her creative potential, Goethe's optimistic attitude can be created.

ATTITUDES AND FUNCTIONS OF A PSYCHOSYNTHESIS COUNSELLOR

Psychosynthesis elaborates several essential attitudes and functions for a counsellor. These can be productive at some stages and limiting at others. The goal is for the psychosynthesis counsellor to have the ability to choose the appropriate attitude or function according to what is congruent with the stage of counselling and presenting issue of the client. No single attitude is right for all clients all the time because counselling is a co-operative interplay between the counsellor and client. This dynamic demands the conscious presence of the counsellor and the ability to orchestrate the various attitudes and functions available.

Accepting

Acceptance is similar to Rogers' concept of unconditional positive regard. Acceptance is the key to establishing an empathic connection with the client which in turn mirrors to the client his or her unique individuality. As Winnicott (1987), a psychoanalyst who recognized the *relational foundation* of being human said, through such mirroring the client will experience that 'when I look I am seen, so I exist'. Rogers used the term 'prizing' the client, meaning that the counsellor accepts whatever the client is or does at any moment. Jewish philosopher Martin Buber (1970) claimed that there are two types of relationships: the I–it relationship and the I–Thou relationship. In the I–it relationship, we relate to others as objects, with expectation, anticipations, imaginings, with structures and borders, which reduces the other to an 'it'. The I–Thou relationship, on the other hand, is one without anticipation, without means and ulterior motives. It is an authentic relationship from centre to centre, which reflects full respect and openness for the being of another person. It is a relationship which is always new, fresh and filled with wonder.

Buber believed that how the other, in this case the client, becomes a Thou is through the disintegration of judgement and expectation. His message is that man becomes an 'I' only through another. This 'other' is the function of acceptance which the counsellor can provide through establishing empathic connection, mentioned above.

In practice, true acceptance from counsellor to client is extremely rare, and although we think we have it, unconsciously some judgement or moralizing easily occurs. Even the most subtle, covert, vague judgement is soon felt by the client and it will invariably damage the positive affirmation through mirroring which is so essential for the client's growth. When such breaks in the empathic connection occur, as they often will, it is vital that the counsellor focuses on reparation of this rupture and the re-establishing of herself as an external unifying centre. The counsellor's ability to disidentify from judication is essential, and she needs to monitor herself with vigilance.

It is easy to accept the client who works well and positively confirms the work, especially when a positive transference exists and the counsellor is seen as an effective helper. Yet the counsellor's capacity for acceptance will be severely tested by certain clients. Examples of such clients are those who are defensive and afraid because of a damaged self-image; are aggressive due to the projection of their own shadow; or are resistant due to a disbelief in the counsellor's authenticity.

A line by a Latin poet says: 'I am a human being and I don't regard anything human as foreign to me.' This line is a good watchword for acceptance as we all regard some behaviours as foreign and would prefer not to address them. A client may present pathology which the counsellor would rather avoid going into. For example, a client who uses physical violence to control her small children, or one who has skilfully hidden her own childhood sexual abuse, may never feel safe enough to reveal her torment if she senses the counsellor's disapprobation. If acceptance is not communicated, these issues cannot be addressed and the therapeutic process will be substantially inhibited. Without acceptance, the client will be afraid of being judged and her darker elements especially will not have the subjective arena necessary for their emergence.

Why is this function of accepting so vital? Acceptance is the initiator for change and the first step of transformation. We will react to or repress anything we do not accept in ourselves. Anything the counsellor does not accept in the client, she, too, will react to or repress. This applies equally to the so-called negative and positive. With acceptance the counsellor models non-judgemental awareness for the client. It is an inclusive awareness which accepts experience as valid, but which recognizes that it is not the whole truth. A response of non-judgemental awareness evokes compassion and acceptance. With acceptance, even if only from the counsellor, a safe environment can be created within which the unacceptable may be embraced. Acceptance precedes fuller awareness which in turn leads to choice.

The foremost way for the counsellor to have the capacity for this level of acceptance is for the counsellor to have established an intra-psychic empathic connection with her own Self. If the counsellor does not have this possibility for self acceptance and positive regard, she will be unable to provide it for another.

There is an additional pay-off for this hard won ability. During the counselling session, if the counsellor feels frustrated, anxious, excited or depressed, something must be triggering these feelings. If the counsellor accepts them as a valid part of the process, she can question what is actually happening at that moment for the client. Through this sensing the counsellor can use her energetic response to the client as an aid to understanding. For example, if during a session the counsellor experiences herself tightening and holding back from the client, she may realize that the client at that moment is deeply afraid of being rejected. If the counsellor has a desire to embrace the client, she may understand that the client actually needs to love herself more and that love from an outside source would not serve her at that moment.

Finally, acceptance of the client's negative feelings can be revolutionary and transformative. Emotions are neither good nor bad, they just are. Negative feelings such as depression, anger or despair are often an appropriate response to a particular life circumstance. The nature of emotional life is that feelings are constantly changing. In a short period of time we may experience a wide range of emotions. Negative emotions, if allowed to exist, will tend to flow with the incessantly changing psychological process of living. However, if feelings are resisted, negatively condemned and excluded from the client's field of awareness, they will persist.

Consequently, it is often our *reaction* to a particular emotion that will keep us stuck, especially if that reaction is negative. Anger is a common example. When feeling angry, many clients will also feel guilty and ashamed of their anger. This judgement will cause it to be pushed away and suppressed. However, that which is suppressed (or repressed) does not sit quietly in the basement, but continues to act upon and colour consciousness. The anger will inevitably find its expression through covert and indirect channels.

To have her anger accepted by the counsellor can surprise the client and enable her to experience that although she feels angry, she is not a bad person. She too may be more able to accept this emotion as a normal human response. It can be deeply affirming for a client to be accepted just as she is, negative emotions and all. Many have never had this experience. Of course it may take time for a counsellor's acceptance to be trusted, which further emphasizes the need for acceptance to be a consistent experience in the relationship with the counsellor.

Knowing and Understanding

Knowing and understanding come hand in hand. It is not possible to understand deeply without first knowing. For the counsellor, knowing is necessary at two levels: first, knowing the details and content of a client's life as a whole and, second, knowing the detailed information around a particular presenting issue.

A prerequisite to fulfilling this function is dialogue and active listening on the part of the counsellor. A counsellor who sees many clients may easily fall prey to superficial knowing, which involves making assumptions about the contents of a client's life. Many human experiences appear to be universal: for example, lack of self-confidence, or anxiety in the face of the unknown, or a need to be loved and accepted may be familiar to the counsellor. When the client presents these more universal experiences, the counsellor may assume familiarity without genuinely using all her care and concern to know this individual. Her problems may appear so similar to the problems of others, yet they are unique.

Knowing requires going thoroughly into the details of a client's life. It is a form of honouring a person, a care that is many times appreciated by the client. Both the depth and the breadth of knowing can greatly enhance understanding. For the counsellor who takes the time to value the details of a client's life, and who remembers this information, communicates her willingness to be present and her trustworthiness. To remember, perhaps months later, that the client's grandmother meant a lot to her, that her secondary school was traumatic or that she lived with an aunt for one year during childhood can communicate a quality of attention that is both nurturing and validating. Assagioli stressed the value of the counsellor knowing things like: what forms of art the client likes, her attitudes towards love, whether she likes sport, her feelings about money and so on. In the early stages of counselling, a psychosynthesis counsellor will spend several sessions gathering this information and facilitating its deeper understanding. This increases the initial assessment and analysis of the client's past and present life situation as well as her difficulties and challenges.

Knowing and information gathering takes place primarily through the medium of dialogue between counsellor and client. A psychosynthesis counsellor, as a matter of course, will invite the client to write an autobiography and will provide guidelines for so doing. This exercise serves both practical and therapeutic functions. It enables the counsellor to get to know the client in more depth and contributes to a higher level of understanding. It also saves time and sessions. Most importantly, it obliges the client to begin to review and reflect on her own life.

There is a further advantage of a qualitative nature. While writing an autobiography, both conscious and unconscious factors are activated which will stimulate further self-awareness. There is often a qualitative difference between the oral and the written information the client will offer. Different aspects of the client's personality emerge through the different media of expression.

According to Assagioli (1965: 71), this knowing on the part of the counsellor, and the psychological assessment it fosters, should include the following elements:

1   the origin of various personality traits;
2   the recognition of existing complexes;
3   the recognition of polarities, ambivalences and conflicts;
4   the recognition of the various 'selves' within;
5   the persistence of traits belonging to preceding psychological ages, i.e. the infantile, adolescent and juvenile.

These same principles apply to knowing at the level of a particular issue or problem that the client may present. Every psychological problem has its biography and larger gestalt which the counsellor needs to be aware of. It is essential for the counsellor to know the history of a presenting issue, as well as its duration. What does she know about its source? What were the circumstances of her life that contributed to its creation? What situations evoke and energize the problem? What environmental factors bring it to the foreground? Are there particular people in the client's life who stimulate the difficulty?

Confirming

'Confirming' can best be described by examples of what it is not. A client comes to see the counsellor having previously been diagnosed as having an obsessive compulsive neurosis. The counsellor replies, 'Well, I don't believe in labels or in cataloguing people. I see you first of all as a human being and we will start with that.' This statement, made with the best of intentions by the counsellor, could be detrimental to the client. It may be a mistake to be overly optimistic and to deny a person's problem. The client also needs to have her pain and pathology acknowledged. Thus, for example, if a client enters counselling deeply depressed and feeling that something is terribly wrong with her life, it would be counterproductive for the counsellor to communicate that her depression is not neurotic and that it is natural to be depressed. The client is likely to feel unconfirmed.

Confirming the client's reality, whatever it may be, serves the function of validating experience. The client's experience *is* reality for her. It warrants being confirmed as her truth for this moment, not to be glossed over by an overly optimistic attitude. This closely relates to the counsellor's fundamental attitude towards pain and suffering. If the counsellor has not reached into her own psyche and uncovered how she deeply feels about pain and suffering, she may deny the client's experience. The counsellor may unconsciously want to *make it better* and work towards its alleviation rather than its transformation.

Viktor Frankl, the founder of Logotherapy, told in a lecture of having gone into a prison to counsel inmates. A behaviourist and a psychoanalyst had preceded him and both in different ways had communicated to the clients that their predicament was not their fault or responsibility. Rather it was because they had had such and such a parent or such and such an upbringing. On the other hand Frankl conveyed to the inmates that, 'It is your fault, it is your responsibility. You made it, you could have avoided it.' This produced a better response from these clients, for Frankl gave them the opportunity to take responsibility. He empowered them for the possibility of change by confirming their reality.

Essentially the counsellor must be willing to enter into the client's phenomenal world. If the task is therapeutic rather than educative, it is vital to use theoretical knowledge without imposing it on the client. In the function of confirming, all psychological jargon and theoretical brilliance must be left behind. The counsellor should respond to her client using language and symbolism which reflects the client's mythology and way of structuring reality rather than the counsellor's professional training. If the client thinks in terms of attachment and detachment, for example, the counsellor can apply these terms to the issue at hand. If the client is religious and uses mystical metaphors, the counsellor can confirm them too.

The counsellor needs to establish a sense of mutuality and an inclusive ambiance. When there is a mutual reality, she will have affirmed the client's experience and communicated her ability to understand. The client is encouraged to open up more by this mutuality. This often occurs easily by means of the counsellor actively listening and mirroring back her understanding to the client.

Non-attachment to Outcome

Non-attachment demands that the counsellor let go of preconceptions and hypotheses regarding what ought to occur in the client's work, as well as the desire for some measurable success. This function is similar to the Eastern concept of karma yoga which stresses working without attachment to the fruits of one's labour. It involves the recognition that ultimately the client is a Self and must be released to her own destiny rather than produce a prescribed result. Metaphorically, the counsellor can offer to the client's own Self the counselling process and place emphasis upon the means for growth rather than the ends. This may inspire the counsellor and client forward and in no way implies not caring for a positive outcome. However, when there is an attachment to that desired outcome, counselling becomes an arena for skilful manipulation.

The counsellor's challenge is to be involved and caring, but not entangled in her understanding and perception. She does not want to limit herself to only one viewpoint. Working for a particular outcome may provide the counsellor with structure and order for the counselling session, but attachment to that outcome may inhibit creative surprises. This function demands that the counsellor be able to embrace uncertainty and welcome the unexpected. Non attachment is possible when the counsellor holds a context in which the client's dilemmas and choices are viewed as evolutionary.

Brown (1983: 45) uses Assagioli's model for the balancing and synthesis of opposites to address the issue of how a counsellor can be involved and yet unattached to results, or at least not let her caring become an obstacle. The synthesis of these two seemingly contradictory attitudes arises from a wider view which:

> trusts the essential unity of life and the unfolding of the individual's growth. From our limited human perspective we do not know if any one outcome is preferable to another. Releasing our clients to their destinies, releases them to take full responsibility for themselves. The client is free because the counsellor is not imposing her idea of what is supposed to happen.

The synthesis of detachment and involvement can only be found by moving to a higher, more encompassing perspective. Here the potential of each polarity may be assumed without compromising the integrity of either. To compromise, with a little involvement and a little detachment, would only reduce the creative tension between these two paradoxical attitudes. Alternatively, to view them from a higher perspective allows for the inclusion of their essence in the counsellor's presence with the client. This is possible when the counsellor trusts that difficulties and choices are evolutionary steps for the client.

Stimulating

In the initial phase of counselling the client takes the counsellor's hand and shows the latter her world, both inner and outer. At a later stage, once the client knows she is accepted and trusts the counsellor, the counsellor can offer her hand, guide the client to other worlds and reveal to her new possibilities. This reflects a more fatherly function, one of showing the client alternative ways forward in her psychospiritual growth.

Stimulating adds an educative function to the counselling relationship. This will take the form of offering, not imposing, an alternative vision, enlarged opportunities, new ideas or psychological principles upon which to reflect, and it will stimulate the client's thinking process. It provides the client with a reframing of her difficulties, creating a new context which determines *how* she perceives the content

Counselling does not need to remain solely on the emotional level. Expanding the client's understanding can enable her to perceive the cause-and-effect mechanism at work. The counsellor and client can reason together about the consequences of certain choices, or the effects of a particular attitude. Elucidating serves the function of making the realities of the client's life more clear and lucid.

As an example, a client may have a strong negative response towards her superior at work. This response may be partially due to her childhood experience of authority figures. She may be on the point of confronting her boss or even resigning from her job. It would be important for the counsellor to explain how past experiences condition current perceptions and distort reality, and to set out for the client the likely consequences of her potential action. A client contemplating a major career change or the termination of a significant relationship would do well to explore the ramifications of alternative choices. To allow such important decisions to be made purely subjectively, without reason, will neither serve the client now, nor will it enhance her ability to be responsible and self-directed in the future.

Connecting

There is a Sufi story of five blind men who were put in front of an elephant, told to touch it and say what it was. The first blind man touched its trunk and said, 'This is clearly a python'. The second touched its leg and said, 'Rubbish, this is a tree trunk'. The third blind man, touching the elephant's side said, 'No, it is a wall'. The fourth felt the elephant's tusk and said, 'This is surely a spear'. The last blind man reached for the tail and defined it as a whip. All the five blind men believed they knew what it was. For each of them, a part of the elephant had been allowed to determine their perception of the whole.

Without degrading the client, she is often like one of these blind men, experiencing a part and losing sight of the whole. This is not a fundamental limitation of the client but rather an inability to see the wood for the trees due to her subjectivity and involvement. It is a part of the counsellor's function to recognize the whole from a more detached perspective. This ability to put the parts together in a meaningful coherent way is the function of connecting.

At an appropriate moment a more holistic vision can be communicated to the client as a hypothesis to be considered. Although it is always more beneficial for her to make discoveries herself, and the insight will be more long lasting, the counsellor may need to serve this function. When, for example, the counsellor notices that the client had the experience of abandonment when she was five, fifteen and thirty, or that her relationship with her employer is similar to her relationship with her father or her childhood head teacher, it may be useful to point it out.

Part of the function of connecting is to confront the obvious. The counsellor will see recurring patterns in the client's life, will see a thread of continuity with certain issues or themes. It is making these connections that gives meaning to the work and helps to integrate the client's process.

The function of connecting also ties the counselling work together in the longer term, over a series of sessions. The client may experience one productive counselling session after another, on seemingly different topics or issues, but at a certain point, it is useful to make connections and find the thread of continuity between these seemingly disparate sessions. The counsellor might for example observe: 'Well last session we worked on your femininity, the one before that we looked at self-assertion, and this time we've explored your relationship with your husband. What's the connection here? Do these themes have anything in common?'

This connecting function fosters 'grounding', which provides the means to bring counselling experiences into other spheres of the client's life, enabling her to apply insights pragmatically. It builds a bridge between the counselling forum and the reality of the client's outer life.

THE THERAPEUTIC STYLE OF THE COUNSELLOR

The therapeutic style of a psychosynthesis counsellor is not necessarily neutral, objective or logical, and requires the full involvement of the counsellor. If the counsellor is to provide a safe, containing and empathic relationship through which the client can heal, all levels of the counsellor's own being must be present in the work. This in turn enables all levels of the client to be validated and included. Deeper, more repressed areas of the client's psyche are welcomed into the arena of counselling. In his investigation of the deeper layers of the unconscious, Jung found images and symbols of a collective character, which he identified as 'archetypes' or universal energies. Assagioli also recognized the value of archetypes, which he defined, in the traditional spiritual sense, as universal principles which unify, heal and give meaning.

In modern psychology there is a tendency to assume that basic human motivation is either love or will. Some theorists say that any behaviour can be traced back to the search for love. Thus, for example, the child who misbehaves in the classroom is trying to get attention, or love. Freud basically believed that we are all seeking a continual sort of union or merging with environment. Eros really refers to this drive for unity which Freud tended to interpret as erotic or sexual.

On the other hand, other psychologists, like Alfred Adler in his Individual Psychology, emphasized the importance of the drive to personal self-assertion or the will to power. He believed that the motivating force beneath behaviour was the thrust continually to dominate, assert and self-express, and that if an individual behaved in a loving way, it was because that was an effective way to get what she wanted. He, too, however, spoke of conflict between the drive for harmony and the drive for autonomy. Karen Horney described the same phenomenon as the opposing drives to move towards others, the need for security, and to move against them, the need for self-assertion.

We could say that these basic energies, so dominant in human behaviour, are reflections of the far-reaching archetypes of love and will. Jung described the two archetypes as two lenses, each of which is equally valid for viewing the human being. Assagioli suggested that the principles of love and will also apply to the counsellor's therapeutic style and presence.

Psychosynthesis regards these two archetypal energies as essential elements in the therapeutic style of the counsellor, ever present in some way in the counselling arena. Any practising counsellor would be wise to understand the dynamic interplay of love and will in their counselling style. There is often a strong tendency in counsellors to attempt to create unity, to prefer being in a state of harmony with the client. This is not unnatural, as a motivating factor for many counsellors is their desire to heal, to care for others and basically to love. The counsellor may easily fall prey to creating this unity by becoming the client's missing half (in terms of love and will), thereby fostering dependency on both sides.

In the training of a psychosynthesis counsellor, the student is led to recognize her innate tendency and to develop its opposite so that both are available as therapeutic styles, according to the needs of the client at any particular moment. No one therapeutic style is appropriate for each client all the time.

What are the therapeutic styles of love and of will? The following terms provide a sense of the difference between the two, but they are neither exhaustive nor absolute.

Love	Will
Universality	Individuality
Consciousness/awareness	Power, change
Feminine principle	Masculine principle
Feelings	Mind
Heart energy	Head energy
Receptive modality	Reflective modality
Being	Doing (becoming)
Mother therapy	Father therapy
Supportive/nourishing	Confrontative/provoking

Love

The archetype or universal energy of *love* carries an awareness of universality, of the interconnectedness of life and subsequent interdependency. Union, unity and harmony between the parts is valued, leading to an expansion of consciousness. In terms of counsellor style it takes the form of an emphasis on the awareness factor and on the client's love needs. The need for security and inclusion is seen to be paramount for the creation of a healthy counselling environment, in which the client feels safe enough to become open and self-disclosing. Consequently the counsellor aims to be receptive, open to the client and her subjective reality.

Especially in the early phases of counselling, this style of 'mother therapy' is vital. As an external unifying centre the counsellor provides the early mirroring that was lacking in the client's early childhood, thus affirming the unique individual human being who exists. The empathic connection the counsellor creates, if successful, is not limited only to moments when the counsellor is physically present with the client, but comes to infuse the 'field' of the client's awareness and offers the required continuity of being. This continuity of being then provides the client with the experience that through it all – the good and the bad, the dark and the light – there is a stable reference point that can accept the fullness of life.

Initially, the counsellor will be the good mother the client never had. She will be unconditionally loving, supporting, nurturing, caring and totally accepting. Her implicit message to the client is, 'you are worthwhile simply because you exist'. With this counsellor style a fine relationship exists between the counsellor and client, one which is subtle, abstract and healing.

This love orientation is one in which the counsellor trusts the beneficence of the unfolding process of the client's work on herself. From a transpersonal perspective which addresses the very essence of being human, the Self, the counsellor will affirm the client's ultimate *fundamental alrightness*. This attitude assumes that the client has within her a unique, hidden blueprint of her overall development. In Eastern psychology it is called 'dharma', the ideal life pattern. The counsellor readily perceives the potential within the client without imposing it in any way, and the client is led to experience that she is OK just as she is.

In Rogerian terms this counselling style is expressly non-directive and non-interventionist. The emphasis is upon the 'heart' and feelings. A non-directive approach traditionally builds a mutual bond and allows the client to find her own answers within. At times, however, clients may find themselves in vicious circles which require more active intervention and direction from the counsellor.

If this therapeutic style is the only choice a counsellor has, she will find that at a certain point, especially after trust has been established, it will become a limitation. The counsellor may well be receptive to the client but not sufficiently responsive. The client may feel secure and safe but the work may remain too abstract with a lack of focus on implementing behavioural changes in the client's everyday life. The counsellor tends to nourish the client but avoids confrontation. There easily can be a lack of boundaries between them and the style becomes too loose and diffused. The client may love to be loved, but will not be stretched and challenged.

It is undeniable that for many clients the experience of being loved and received is already immensely therapeutic. However, the counsellor may find herself *following* the client around during sessions, with little progress being made. A distortion of this style is a tendency for the counsellor to avoid taking responsibility for the work and to fear intervening when appropriate, perhaps out of her oversensitivity to the client. Clearly there are times when more definition and decisiveness are called for.

Will

The archetype or energy of Will is a very different story. When this is active, the emphasis naturally shifts towards fostering a strong identity and the emergence of inherent individuality. The client increasingly internalizes the external unifying centre of the counsellor, and an *intra-psychic empathic relationship* grows. Little by little, the client learns to provide for herself what the counsellor until now, has provided for her. This important shift comprises the emergence of an *internal unifying centre* which is the gateway to fundamental health and well-being. The journey to an internal unifying centre occurs throughout the course of counselling, provided that *empathic failures* between the counsellor and client are processed well. In this sense then, the client learns the capacity to *hold* the good and the bad, the successes and the failures in one totality of experience with an awareness that knows her identity is not dependent upon either – she still remains herself throughout.

The counsellor is orientated decidedly towards change and the healthy development and dynamic use of volition. The client is encouraged to find and own her personal power with high value placed on autonomy and independence. In this modality the counsellor adopts a more mental and reflective way of relating to the client. Change, the value of change and the importance of becoming are implicit.

Assagioli called this therapeutic style 'father therapy', as the counsellor fulfils a healthy fatherly function. She models sound challenging behaviour and sometimes becomes provocative. She may challenge the client to look deeper, take greater risks and more positive steps forward. With certain issues it is appropriate to confront and encourage the client to go beyond her self-imposed limitations. The counsellor stimulates the pursuit of goals. She opens the client's perspective, and reminds her of what she is capable of. She may include the educative function, providing maps and models relevant to the client's process. There is more use of structure and techniques designed to provoke transformation.

This therapeutic style is more directive, with the counsellor assuming substantial responsibility for the client's work. For example, she maintains a clear, concrete plan of where the work is going. The implicit message from counsellor to client is, 'Yes, you can take that step, you can improve and grow.' This ability to intervene and give guidance to the client, when appropriate, can valuably *contain* the counselling work. The client definitely feels she is in safe and capable hands.

However, this therapeutic style, too, if used exclusively, has its limitations. While the counsellor provides the right direction at the right moment and has fine mental clarity – the client may abdicate responsibility to her. The client may perceive the counsellor as a teacher, an authority figure, with the obvious danger of fostering dependency. This style can be too imposing and directive and runs the risk of tearing down the client's defences prematurely. When this happens, the client has a tendency to slip back to the previous stage of growth and to use her defences with renewed vigour.

Given the emphasis on structure, maps and models, the counsellor will be as limited as these structures. If all she has is a hammer, she will only see nails. If her tools are diverse and flexible there will be no problem, but if they are limited and sparse clients will be made to fit the tools rather than the tools serve the client. This tendency to use solely a more directive, structured style of counselling has been described as morphophilic, the love of form.

Synthesis

The synthesis of the two archetypes, love and will, in the counsellor's style is called 'presence'. Presence requires the counsellor to have both of these valuable resources available. For the counsellor to have the ability to support and nourish, and to provide direction firmly means both trusting the process and creating the process. It means the counsellor having available her mind and her feelings, her receptivity and her ability to reflect and stimulate.

It is the responsibility of each psychosynthesis counsellor to choose an appropriate therapeutic style for her own personality and temperament, and for that of her clients, while remaining aware of this broader context of love and will. The counsellor's presence is primarily non-verbal and is not made explicit to the client. It is more an attitude and way of being with the client.

The Client's Therapeutic Style

However, there is another person present – the client. It is useful for the counsellor to notice whether the client is seeking love or will when she arrives for each session and presents her psychological process. However clients, too, will habitually identify with one or the other style and attitude towards themselves and their difficulties in life.

The polarity of will   A client may be quite harsh on herself, constantly challenging herself to do better, grow more and move faster. She may be demanding with rigid goals for the work. She exerts upon herself a pressure to change, and will have structured and planned how this should happen. Her boundaries with particular psychological issues are very tight and inflexible. She is unable to find compassion for her own suffering and has unrealistic demands and expectations of herself and others.

Confronted by a client with this attitude, the natural tendency of the counsellor is to become more passive and receptive: after all this client knows what she wants and where she wants to go. Further, the counsellor wouldn't dream of adding yet more will to the relationship herself. For example, a client who has an excessive self-critic and who is very hard on herself tends to evoke the counsellor's compassion. The counsellor herself becomes more soft and loving. However, polarizing with the client's stance may only reinforce this rigid and imbalanced stance. The counsellor would be likely to end up following the client around her tightly structured plan.

The counsellor is in danger of giving up her own discriminatory capacities when faced with a client who is motivated and energetic in her presentation. This natural tendency for the counsellor to polarize her therapeutic style with that of the client has to be carefully watched.

By becoming more passive and receptive (the love archetype) the counsellor would establish a unit with the assertive client. She would become the client's missing half. In the above example, the counsellor might adopt the 'underdog' position and try to facilitate the client becoming more soft, allowing and accepting of herself and her limitations. This is all well and good except that it is the counsellor who is doing the work of being the opposite for the client. She is providing what is lacking rather than the client finding a more loving way of being within herself. So between counsellor and client we end up with two halves of the whole and unity is created. But it is at the expense of individual wholeness.

The polarity of love   Exploring the love-orientated client's stance we find a similar pattern. For example, if a client presents her issue with a style of low energy, low motivation and is unwilling to take responsibility, she is in effect saying to the counsellor 'Fix me, you know what to do.' This attitude draws the counsellor into adding the opposite: taking charge, giving direction and getting the process moving with statements like, 'Let's work on this, and in such and such a way.' Although this *rescues* the client and helps her to get going, it also means that the counsellor is providing what is missing for her. The counsellor would again be polarizing with the client. Again we have achieved unity but by two halves making the whole rather than the client being facilitated to find her own capabilities and resources.

The solution   Due to the compensatory function of the unconscious, whatever attitude or stance the client may take, its opposite will be evoked in her unconscious. Her unconscious will be trying to bring about balance and it has the best opportunity to do so if the counsellor is not providing it for the client. If, for example, the client is passive and resigned to an isolated existence with little social contact, there will be a place in her psyche which will not accept this unhealthy state. Her unconscious will seek to compensate by giving her messages, dreams and impulses to take action to change this predicament. This healthy balancing function in the client's own psyche needs to be evoked and fostered, rather than the counsellor providing what is missing.

The solution is for the counsellor more or less to match the love–will balance of the client. If the client is very wilful and assertive, the counsellor too can take a more active and directing role. If the client is very passive and immobilized, the counsellor can take a receptive, non-directive stance. In terms of these two archetypes, love and will, this style will tend to evoke from within the client what is needed to make her whole. It will evoke the client's love and will, her ability to love and accept herself *and* to know that she can grow and change, that she can trust the process and take responsibility for her life.

If the client is very passive and unmotivated, the counsellor can ask questions like, 'Well, what do you want to do about this?' or 'What do you see going on here?' or 'What alternatives do you have?' or 'How do you want to deal with this?' These probings evoke the client's will and her motivation to take responsibility for the issue.

Alternatively, if the client is already extremely wilful and demanding of herself, the counsellor can guide her in a way that is also wilful such as challenging her position and provoking her compassion and acceptance of herself.

Obviously, none of the above process is stated explicitly. It manifests through the counsellor's attitude, style and way of being with the client. This is not a static procedure, but a co-operative interplay, a flowing dance which requires conscious alertness from the counsellor. Clients may live predominantly in one polarity, love or will, and the evocation of the missing opposite can take a long time. This would be the case, for instance, with a client who grew up in an authoritarian environment where achievement, autonomy and performance were highly valued. There is a strong pattern in such a client where love and self-nurturing were chronically absent.

Clients may adopt different polarities in response to different situations and in different intrapersonal dynamics. In her relationships with men, a client might settle for less than she deserves because she has taken the position that women are not supposed to be demanding. Here her will may be sorely lacking while at work she might be an absolute tyrant. The appropriate therapeutic style is different depending on which life circumstance the client is presenting.

The main point is that there is a strong unconscious drive in the counsellor towards unity, leading to the tendency to fill in the client's missing half, whereas the need is for the client's missing half to be evoked, so that she can be whole. Otherwise the unity created by the counsellor polarizing with the client is regressive. Neither the counsellor nor the client is operating from a position of wholeness, with their own love and their own will available.

Having explored in depth the counsellor and her role in psychosynthesis counselling, we now turn our attention to its tools and techniques. Psychosynthesis integrates principles and techniques into a broad framework designed to foster evolution towards increasing personal and spiritual development. The psychosynthesis counsellor will have a wide range of methods available, according to the needs of the client.

3

BASIC TECHNIQUES OF
PSYCHOSYNTHESIS COUNSELLING

In his formulation of psychosynthesis, Assagioli intentionally created an open system – a skeleton upon which counsellors and psychotherapists could further elaborate. Rather than handing down a finished product or doctrine, he offered them his vision and encouragement to explore a large number of avenues and methods. Consequently it is the responsibility of the pyschosynthesis counsellor to choose appropriate therapeutic techniques. The work may be on any level – physical, emotional, mental, imaginative – and the counsellor must master all these modes in order to have a wide range of techniques available.

Assagioli intended psychosynthesis to be centred in life rather than in the clinic or in the laboratory. He envisaged it to assist clients to understand and master their problems, actively shape their lives, improve their relationships and increase meaning and purpose. Although the counsellor is aware that the client is ultimately responsible, she will offer choices about the ways they might work.

EXPERIENTIAL WORK

Active dialogue and discussion are appropriate for understanding psychological problems, and awareness of harmful images and complexes may help to disintegrate them, but do not necessarily produce positive change. For many psychological issues, the *cognitive* aspect needs to be complemented with *experiential* techniques, designed to evoke and explore deeper unconscious levels. The psychosynthesis approach is primarily pragmatic and existential. Although the overall goals and perspective are similar among practitioners, the methods they employ may vary considerably.

Experiential work can uncover the historical roots of a problem as well as the creative possibility for change. It uses different modalities to work on an issue – the body and sensations, the emotions, the imagination and the intellect. The more modalities from which the counsellor has to choose, the deeper and more productive the counselling will be. For example, guided imagery, described below, may be used to bring to the surface unhappy childhood experiences; or emotional abreaction can release repressed feelings. For some clients, physical expression can mobilize psychological energy and enable them to go beyond dysfunctional behaviour.

BALANCING AWARENESS AND WILL

Given that the indiscriminate use of experiential techniques is not advisable, how does the counsellor discern when to work experientially or when active dialogue is appropriate? Every method or technique should be subordinate to the client's needs, the phase of treatment and her basic temperament. The psychosynthesis practitioner must learn to discriminate wisely.

Although Assagioli contended that psychoanalytical treatment is inadequate to bring about true integration and growth, the danger exists, with the use of experiential techniques, of the counsellor becoming merely a technician. The skilful use of techniques can never be a substitute for, or be used as an avoidance of, the human relationship. In fact, no technique will succeed if there is not a therapeutic relationship which provides for the client an *empathic holding relationship* in which the client feels seen and safe. The dynamic of transference and countertransference is paramount. The transferred childhood pattern, which clients unconsciously *live again* in the relationship with their counsellor, takes primacy for attention. It is through addressing the transferred childhood pattern that the counsellor can further provide the essential *mirroring* the client needs in order that the past may be redeemed and her internal reference point affirmed. She can experience that it is possible to transcend archaic ways of relating through authentic relating with the therapist. Also, if a negative transference exists, the use of a technique could provide a forum for increased resistance; on the other hand, a positive transference can enhance its effectiveness. Assagioli (1965: 67) issued the following warning:

> This danger can, and we hope will, be offset: first by the very multiplicity and variety of the techniques which prevents giving undue importance to any one of them; second, by the steady cultivation and use of the synthetic spirit, by the constant endeavour to keep the entire picture in view, to relate always the part to the whole; last by emphasizing in theory and in practice the central, decisive importance of the human factor, of the living interpersonal relationship between the therapist and patient.

Another guideline for the counsellor, when discriminating the verbal versus experiential method, is to observe the balance between the client's inner experience and outer behaviour, between awareness and will. Experiential techniques, such as guided imagery, expand the client's awareness and provide her with more insight, but awareness by itself may not be curative. The client's use of her will actively to change must complement her awareness. A client can for instance be 'aware' that every time she speaks to her mother she is filled with anxiety and resentment. She can become aware of *why* she feels this way – because her mother is judgemental and unaccepting – but this awareness may not alter her experience. The missing factor is her volition and choice to act. Experiential work is often necessary to release emotions and blocked energies, but a point may be reached when the client needs active dialogue in order to release her history.

On the other hand, a client may be imbalanced by an excess of will, which is to say, she may operate as if it is only necessary to *do* something about her difficulties. She may have it *all worked out* and, in the above example, may think the answer lies solely in severing contact with her mother or refusing to discuss certain issues with her, not realizing that she carries her mother around inside her. For her the answer lies in a more experientially orientated *working things through*, which provides a broader consciousness.

The process of expanding awareness, integrating what is foreground and evoking behavioural change was described by Assagioli (1965: 99) as 'fractional analysis'. He wrote: 'the quantity of analysis, of exploration of the unconscious, is relatively limited . . . and care is taken that the varied quota, or amount of energy released from the unconscious into the conscious is immediately dealt with – cautiously; it is controlled, transmuted or utilized through expression'. In other words, for effective change to occur, there must be a synthesis of *experience and understanding*. Understanding alone may be helpful but not transformative. But only experiencing the subjective state may be equally limiting. When understanding and experience are interwoven the results are far reaching.

Catharsis

Catharsis, clinically known as abreaction, may occur at any moment in the counselling session. Catharsis essentially means 'the process of becoming pure'. The client can experience a physical, emotional or mental catharsis which takes her to the *purity of things*. As a means of healing, a psychosynthesis counsellor will encourage catharsis in order to release previously repressed or blocked psychological energy. Negative emotions, when consistently suppressed and unexpressed, will tend to dampen our quality of aliveness, possibly lead to psychosomatic difficulties and contribute to neurotic perceptions of self and others.

In combination with other techniques, the psychosynthesis counsellor will encourage a release of energy, be it through verbal expression, emotional abreaction (through crying or expression of feelings) or physical action. This enables the client to perceive and experience with a less distorted awareness, in order to create a right sense of proportion and liberate her.

This process is not just a throwing out of negative affect in order to get rid of it, but is a purifying, refining and transmuting of subjective energy to its more essential form. The client will still have the negative emotion available as an appropriate response, but will not be controlled by it.

To the psychosynthesis counsellor catharsis is not seen as an *end*, but requires a further step, through actively seeking to replace the previously negative state with something positive and transformative. This involves the client's will and her choice to implement behavioural changes which are congruent with the insight or learning gained. This creative work goes beyond the distortion which has crept into some areas of humanistic psychology, namely catharsis for its own sake and as a goal in itself.

TECHNIQUES

Many practical techniques are utilized in psychosynthesis counselling. Among them are relaxation, concentration, catharsis, critical analysis, psychological journal, body movement, subpersonality work, balancing and synthesis of opposites, gestalt dialogue, symbolic art work and free drawing, ideal models, self-identification, inner dialogue, mental imagery and the use of symbols, meditation and creative expression. Eight of the most commonly used techniques, their indications and contra-indications are described below.

Critical Analysis

Critical analysis is a discursive method which can be used to assess both the blocks and potentials of the personality, and to initiate an exploration of the unconscious in order to reach the roots of psychological complexes. Critical analysis additionally provides a forum which supports the counsellor as the client's external unifying centre, and allows the therapeutic relationship to build towards one of empathic understanding and concern. Through this dialogue the counsellor communicates to the client a relational sense of being, an abiding alrightness. Critical analysis can evoke creative understanding and often catharsis. Through active dialogue the counsellor encourages the client to use her mind, with observation and discrimination, to bring clearly into her consciousness the irrational elements of her problems and corresponding feelings. The counsellor intends her to see the drawbacks and harm to herself and others of their uncontrolled manifestation.

Through critical analysis, for example, a client with self-destructive tendencies was able to trace these feelings to childhood and discovered many experiences where her self-esteem had been damaged. She saw how she had translated these negative experiences into self-hatred. She further realized how her self-hatred not only caused her unconsciously to wish to hurt herself, but had also transformed into passive aggression. With these discoveries she was able to change her self-destructive behaviours.

Critical analysis is indicated when the client is largely unaware of her psychological and subjective history, and whenever there is an excess of affective energies and dysfunctional behaviours. It also allows for a moment of reflection or mental consideration of a situation before acting. This technique would be contra-indicated for clients who over-intellectualize and might misuse the technique for unhealthy suppression of

emotions. Clients who are already extremely self-critical would not benefit, as the technique could foster an excessively judgemental attitude. This
could have negative implications for the client herself and could cause her
to direct her aggression towards others.

Psychological Journal

With this technique subjective reflection and writing is used, through
keeping a psychological journal or workbook. This is similar to Progoff's
Intensive Journal work and has been adapted to psychosynthesis by
Martha Crampton (1969). The use of the technique begins with the client
writing an autobiography, and continues with the client recording her
inner life and its developments as they occur. Although the focus should
be on her unfolding awareness of herself, and on the steps forward she is
able to take, outer events may be recorded to set the inner events in context.

There are several purposes for using this technique. Most importantly,
it enables the client to learn to formulate her thoughts, feelings and obser-
vations with greater clarity, thus enhancing self-awareness. The choice to
write implies a further commitment to change, and if there is a problem to
be solved or an area of confusion to be sorted out, writing can help to
define and initiate its resolution. This technique also stimulates the creative process and releases dormant insights.

Keeping a psychological journal also has a cathartic benefit. It allows
the client to release, in a harmless way, powerful negative emotions, which
could be disruptive if outwardly expressed. It provides a means of dis-
charging tensions, and of becoming aware of their underlying meaning, as
well as giving 'symbolic satisfaction' to the unconscious.

The psychological journal may have sections in any of the following
areas:

- *dialogue with ideas*: any area of vital intellectual interest in which the
  client is trying to advance her understanding;
- *dialogue with persons*: insights into or questions about relationships;
- *dialogue with events*: the client's response to meaningful events in her
  life;
- *inner dialogues*: miscellaneous thoughts, musings, intuitions or questions which do not fit under other headings;
- *dreams*: description, context, associations and amplifications of the
  client's night dreams;

53

- *imagery*: visualizations or experiences of other sensory modalities, including those which come spontaneously or while using a mental-imagery technique;
- *identity*: notes on the client's sense of personal identity, experiences with meditative techniques related to the question of essential being;
- *will*: notes on the client's experience with using her will, evaluation of areas of strength and weakness;
- *peak experiences*: accounts of any high or deep superconscious experiences of peace, joy, love, expansion, awakening and their circumstances and effects;
- *problems*: areas which the client would like to change by working on them in counselling. This includes her own assessment of her difficulties and results of previous attempts to resolve them.

The technique of a psychological journal can be used by anyone with the willingness to invest the required time in reflection and introspection, and by those sincerely interested in their psychological and spiritual development. However, for obsessive–compulsive types who might misuse the technique by *over-writing* in an unconscious and unproductive way, it is not recommended.

Mental Imagery

Imagery is the language of the unconscious and reveals in a symbolic way conflicts and contents which may be unavailable to the conscious self. Mental imagery provides a means of communication with the vast reservoir of the unconscious, and of expanding awareness in a particular area. Through imagery the myth-making capacity of the human mind has the opportunity for creating stories and events which pictorially represent the client's inner reality.

The imagination follows no rules of reality. All sorts of imagery may emerge of natural or artificial landscapes, people and beasts, demons and healing entities, and at times cosmic and visionary scenarios. The counsellor often suggests that the client give these images the power of speech and movement, and impossible things may happen, illogical and irrational stories unfold, inanimate objects come alive.

The psychosynthesis counsellor primarily uses mental imagery in one of two ways, or in combination: *evocatively* by drawing out that which already exists in the unconscious, and by consciously choosing to *recondition* the psyche with images which are positive, and developmentally progressive. In evocative imagery work, no predetermined images are suggested, but rather the client is invited to 'call up' a visual image for a specific purpose. This may take the form of inviting the client to allow an image to emerge for a particular problem or life situation, or in answer to a question asked by the counsellor.

With mental imagery the creative myth-making, story-telling function of the unconscious is at work. For example, when invited to evoke an image for her difficulty with self-assertion, a client visualized a bear in a cage, angry and bellowing loudly. The client instantly recognized this as her fear of her own power which could be destructive and therefore needed to be caged. The bear, too, was an accurate symbol of the undeveloped state of her capacity for self-assertion. She was invited to speak with the bear to get to know it better, and to find out what was needed for its liberation. The bear communicated its need for nourishment and small forages into the environment. To her surprise the client discovered that the cage was not locked and the only thing blocking her was her own fear. This realization led to intensive work with childhood experiences where her aggression was thwarted and subsequently repressed. Through the imagery, both the source of the problem and its resolution were discovered.

Evocative imagery often leads to abreaction (catharsis) and the reliving of repressed memories and fixations. The counsellor encourages full emotional response and the client is helped to 'work through' disturbing experiences and conflicts on a symbolic level. Once the client has 'lived' something on the symbolic level, the counsellor encourages the client's interpretation from her own experience, rather than it being imposed from an outside source. Symbolically facing a difficult or threatening situation and working it through provides the client with an expanded sense of possibilities which replace immature and neurotic ways of feeling and relating. Essential in this process is the counsellor helping the client to bridge what happened in the imagery work to her attitudes and real-life situation.

With the *reconditioning* use of imagery, the counsellor offers selected images to be used by the client in order to set into motion chosen psychological processes. Assagioli (1965: 144) suggested a psychological principle which says that 'every image has in itself a motor drive or tendency and images and mental pictures tend to produce the physical conditions and external acts corresponding to them'. If we are conditioned by our imaginings, the structured and positive use of chosen images allows for the creation of their corresponding psychological state.

Symbols are accumulators of psychic energy and carry a qualitative energy, with a dynamic relationship existing between the symbol and the reality it represents.

The use of this form of imagery calls for the counsellor to suggest that the client create an image or symbol, again for a specific purpose. It can be a positive symbol which has been produced by the client herself in dreams, fantasy, mental imagery or one which has been chosen by the counsellor from the field of universally valued symbols. Crampton (1969: 5) cites examples of the latter as:

> symbols of integration around a central core (mandalas, a lotus, a radiant body like a star or sun); symbols of inner wisdom (a wise old being, with whom the client can enter into dialogue, as a means of evoking inner guidance); symbols of growth and transformation (like the blossoming of a rose, the cycle of a tree, the metamorphosis from cocoon to butterfly); or symbols of constructive human relationships (the enactment of a positive step in a difficult relationship, a visualization of the capacity for intimacy, or climbing a mountain with a loved one).

The reconditioning effect of mental imagery is based on the analogous qualities between the symbol and reality and, when analysed, rich insights are available. It can also be used to strengthen and develop latent qualities, strengths and skills.

Perhaps more than any other technique, mental imagery has strong contra-indications, which require the counsellor's respect. With clients who may be psychotic or borderline it should never be used. With those lacking any solid sense of identity it must be used with caution. The danger in both cases is the risk of stirring up too much material from the unconscious when the personality is incapable of integrating it. For this type of client there is already an excessive amount of free-flowing images, and imagery work would only add to the chaos when order, structure and integration are sorely needed.

Assagioli (1965: 189) also stressed caution with clients who already have an over-active imagination and for whom symbolism is the line of least resistance. These types probably already have an over-production of symbols. For such individuals imagery would offer a further escape from reality and a substitution for normal life. With extremely introverted psychoneurotics, mental imagery may be used, but with discretion and with emphasis on bridging the imagery to outer reality.

Although initially difficult due to a weakness of the imaginative function, with more intellectually orientated clients, mental imagery can be extremely valuable. This is also true for overly extroverted clients who have very little symbolic activity. Once accustomed to the technique, such clients find imagery work a valuable means of communication with their unconscious. Generally speaking, imagery is a productive tool for most 'healthy neurotics'.

Singer (1973: 103) stresses the breadth and scope of imagery work:

> Active imagination is, more than anything else, an attitude toward the unconscious. It cannot be said to be a technique or even a method of coming to terms with the unconscious, because it is a different experience for each person who is able to use it. The common feature of all varieties of active imagination is its dependence upon a view of the unconscious that recognizes its contents as containing innate structures (archetypes) which inevitably define the potentialities and the limitations of the personality.

Free Drawing

Free drawing is a technique of psychosynthesis that can be used by almost every client, often with surprising results. The act of drawing, choosing colours, shapes and lines can provide a channel for the client to express both positive and negative subjective states. It entices the unconscious, which in certain respects has primitive and archaic traits, to express itself freely. As with mental imagery, it builds a bridge between the conscious self and unconscious contents, between the rational mind and its more irrational intuitive elements. It offers a medium of expression for releasing repressed psychological energy.

There are two ways of using the technique:

1 *The spontaneous method*: This involves the client 'playing' with paper and coloured crayons, allowing the hands to move freely without thought. The best attitude is simply to 'let it happen', to see what will emerge. If full and free expression of emotion is allowed, much negative energy can be released.

2 *Symbolic art work*: The client may be invited to draw her sense of, and feelings about, a particular symbol received during mental imagery work. These pictures need not be precisely reproduced; the subjective state they represent is therapeutically useful. The meaning hidden in

colour and shape, and the feelings evoked, bring learning and insight. When using this type of free drawing it is essential to stress that it has nothing to do with being artistic.

As with any experiential technique, it is revealing for counsellor and client to spend time analysing and interpreting the meaning of the free drawing. Emphasis is always placed upon the client's subjective interpretation. The technique of free drawing is harmless and may be applied to any client who is not blocked by the use of crayons and paper.

Disidentification and Self-identification

A sense of identity is crucial to the feeling of being alive, and the search for identity is fundamental to human experience. Identity is more than a conglomeration of current psychosocial traits. There is in each individual an 'I', an observing centre of awareness and volition which transcends psychosocial identity. In the process of psychosynthesis counselling the client becomes aware that within her are many more or less conscious aspects, roles and attitudes with which from time to time she becomes identified.

More specifically, the normal state for most of us is to be identified with that which at any one moment gives the greatest sense of aliveness, positive or negative, and which seems most real. This partial identification may be temporarily satisfying, but has serious drawbacks. For example, the client dominated by anxiety or depression, by aggression or ambition is enslaved by a limited consciousness. From time to time we all have felt ourselves imprisoned by oppressive psychological patterns which appear to be beyond our control. This limited identification decreases our ability to identify with many other aspects of our personality, to use and enjoy them.

A basic tenet of psychosynthesis is that we are dominated by everything with which our self is identified. We can dominate and control, in a regulatory sense, everything from which we disidentify ourselves. The process of identification is universal and can be reversed only by its opposite, disidentification. The technique of disidentification enables us consciously to detach ourselves from the various aspects of our personality. The experience of a deeper sense of personal identity is known in psychosynthesis as the 'I'. The experience of being centred can create inner freedom and open us to more of our creative potential.

Disidentification can enable the client to influence and regulate the spontaneous flow of psychological states. This notion corresponds to the concept of personal responsibility, the idea that we can direct our lives. The freedom to choose appropriate personal responses comes in large measure through disidentifying from that which is not essential, and through identification with a deeper centre of being,

The technique of disidentification can be used in counselling primarily in two ways. The counsellor can encourage the client to disidentify from negative or limiting identities, beliefs, attitudes, behaviours, emotions or roles. For example, the client who is in crisis because her children have grown up and left home may be encouraged to recognize that she is essentially more than a mother. A client identified with a damaging self-image can become aware of the limiting effect of this and choose to identify with her strengths. A client overwhelmed by feelings of despair or aggression can disidentify and discover alternative responses.

Disidentification as a technique, the *self-identification exercise*, will be introduced to the client when the counsellor feels she is ready. Consistent use of the technique builds a psychological skill which develops with practice. Having the ability to disidentify enables the client to expand her perspective at will, and is invaluable in the creation of a stable sense of identity and is the first step towards experience of the Self.

According to Assagioli, the principle and technique of disidentification and self-identification should be used as early as possible, as it is fundamental to psychological health. Its use is indicated particularly with clients who are imprisoned by limited identifications. The technique also defends against the constant stream of influences and psychological content, both inner and outer, which may not be appropriate.

However, not every client has the psychological capacity to grasp the principle and technique, in which case the counsellor will have to wait until a later stage. The use of any technique may be inappropriate when a client is experiencing emotional turmoil. The greatest contra-indication here, as with mental-imagery work, is with borderline psychotics, with whom the technique could lead to depersonalization. It should be used with caution for clients whose obsessive introspective tendencies outweigh their active participation in life.

Procedure   The procedure for using this technique consists of directing the mind's eye, or observing function, upon the world of psychological experience and content of which we can become aware. We can direct our field of observation to our subjective experience of physical sensation and bodily experience, emotional states and mental activities.

The first field of observation is physical sensation and bodily experience. This leads to an awareness of how our body is constantly changing, both in terms of physical well-being and developmental processes. Objective observation of the flow of bodily sensation fosters the realization that our self is not our body, not a conglomerate of physical experience. We *have* a body which is constantly changing.

The second field of observation is the affective realm of feelings and emotions. Here too, we easily realize that our feelings are constantly changing. One moment we feel one emotion – the next, a different one. Our range of emotional experience is vast. Certain feelings have a greater hold on our consciousness, yet we can become aware that we *have* these feelings.

The third field of observation is that of mental activity and our thought processes. Here too, we find a multitude of diverse elements – opinions, ideas, beliefs, attitudes, philosophies. Mental activity is also changing, fleeting and varied. Yet there is someone in us who thinks, or *has* thoughts.

Finally, having observed and acknowledged these three realms of experience, we may also recognize that we *have but are not* any of them. Ultimately we are a *self* who *has* the rich resources of body sensations, emotional experience and mental activities, which are instruments of experience, perception and action. Assagioli (1965: 117) tells us:

> the 'I' is simple, unchanging, constant and self-conscious. The experience of the 'I' can be formulated as follows: I am I, a centre of pure consciousness. To state this with conviction does not mean that one has reached the experience of the 'I', but it is the way which leads to it. It is the key to, and the beginning of, the mastery of our psychological processes.

Ideal Model

The ideal-model technique involves the counsellor helping the client uncover or create an idea, sense or vision of what is possible, by evoking 'potential' from whatever level the client is working. It is based on the counsellor's trust that the client can find her own constructive answers, and a positive way forward. This may be achieved through active dialogue, mental imagery or free drawing.

The technique of ideal model may be used in three principal ways. First, in its *problem-related usage*, it can serve to foster the client's experiential discovery of the potential contained within a problem and to envision its resolution or transformation. When oppressed by a psychological problem, the client may experience a lack of motivation and hopelessness. In such a case this technique evokes volition and builds a positive image and provides a model of how to reach the envisioned state. In short, the client builds an image of herself living freely without the difficulty. For example, the client who imagined a caged bear representing her power can imagine symbolically liberating the bear and can build an ideal model of herself using power in her life in creative and constructive ways.

Second, we have the *cultivation of the opposite*. In order to break psychological 'vicious circles', the ideal-model technique can be used to cultivate a desired quality or affective state. This idea, based on a principle of the Yoga Sutras, is that a problem cannot be solved at its own level; its opposite must be cultivated. A client overwhelmed by fear and anxiety may cultivate courage; one imprisoned by rage can develop compassion; a client lost in self-depreciation may learn to love herself.

The ideal-model technique is not the same as 'positive thinking', nor is it meant to be a substitute for the counsellor and client actively and directly confronting difficult issues. It is most effective when used to complement such work. It also ensures that counselling is more than merely going into pain and negativity; it offers an expanded vision and the promise of a regenerated outcome.

Third, *overall direction and purpose* is the use of the ideal-model technique which most often applies to the later stages of counselling, when the client's urgent foreground issues have been addressed. Clients who are tormented by their suffering are unable to respond to the evocation of potential, and their pain warrants immediate response.

According to the Eastern doctrine of dharma, there is an ideal life pattern for each of us, a blueprint implicit in our psyche. Psychosynthesis also holds that such a *purpose* exists in the higher unconscious and the client may discover it through the use of the ideal-model technique. In an evolutionary sense, this dharma represents the direction of the client's progressive unfoldment, and there are steps along the way to the realization of this ideal pattern. The ideal model is not an abstract norm derived from outside authorities, nor is it a tyrannical or impersonal standard of some impractical and unreachable goal. It is eminently personal, realistic and consequently attainable.

The ideal-model technique provides a positive thrust to counselling and expands the context within which an exploration of the unconscious, the catharsis of repressed emotions and the treatment of symptoms takes place. It reframes counselling, to include the client's exploration of life purpose, eliminating obstacles to it and facilitating its realization.

Assagioli saw the ideal-model technique as an important step in all psychotherapeutic procedures and consequently it is universally indicated. He stressed, however, that in working with the imagination, the negative must be addressed before the progressive and desired good may come about, although the desired good may be kept in mind. With any of its three uses, this technique is most effective when the client is capable of perceiving and experiencing beyond the immediate emotional charge of an issue. Often it is necessary first to confront the client's problem *head on*, for her to experience it *as it is* and embrace the difficulty. If this is not done, psychological forces within her, which run counter to the constructive tendencies, could evoke resistances.

The ideal-model technique is contra-indicated with clients who are victim to an excessive superego or internal critic. In such cases, the ideal model could be used as a yardstick to criticize and further deepen the superego's unrealistic demands. The client must have the possibility of using the ideal model as a vision of what she may become rather than as a psychological weapon with which to reprimand herself. With this type of client it is wiser to improve self-image before using the technique.

Grounding and Creative Expression

The step beyond insight and understanding consists of enabling the seeds of change to come to full bloom. Although significant work occurs in the counselling setting, it is only part of the client's growth. No vision, however deep and beautiful, is truly valid unless it is anchored in personal expression and woven into the fabric of everyday life.

With emphasis on personal responsibility, the psychosynthesis counsellor encourages the client to continue her *work* between sessions, to ensure that the growth attained on the psychological level is applied in concrete and practical ways. The counsellor helps the client to choose specific activities between sessions, which serve the purpose of deepening and elaborating her insights and provide a means of actualizing them, by fostering behavioural change in everyday life.

Often the grounding emerges quite naturally from the work of a session, and creates the opportunity for the client to take volitional action. It frequently involves dealing with obstacles in interpersonal relationships and cultivating chosen skills and qualities. For instance, a client who was learning to assert herself chose to make one daily act of assertion and report it back to the counsellor. Another client, who was improving communication skills, determined to express an honest feeling to one of her colleagues.

Many of the techniques referred to in this chapter can also be applied to the client's daily life: psychological journal keeping, the self-identification exercise, meditation on an ideal model and so on. Ideally the grounding is *created* by the client and reflects her will to take responsibility for her life. It can be undertaken in minor ways through small actions, or it can be a step-by-step enactment of a major modification of behaviour.

The Gestalt Approach

Psychosynthesis integrates principles and techniques into a broad framework designed to facilitate the natural human drive towards development. As each client is unique, the psychosynthesis counsellor will have a wide range of methods, and choose the one best suited for each client. Consequently the breadth of psychosynthesis allows it to embrace other psychological schools and incorporate their methods when appropriate. Aspects of the gestalt therapy are frequently used in psychosynthesis counselling.

Simply put, gestalt is an integrative approach to counselling, rooted in an existential orientation. For a full description of this fine psychology see the 'Counselling in Action' series text, *Gestalt Counselling in Action* (Clarkson, 1999).

Within the Gestalt approach, two principles and their ensuing therapeutic techniques are primarily used. First, there is *experiencing 'what is'*: gestalt therapy maintains that the awareness needed for identifying imbalances and working them through is contained within the present moment-to-moment experience. Emphasis is placed upon experiencing *what is* rather than talking *about* it, conceptualizing, repressing or denying it and distancing or sedating oneself from the existential moment.

The counsellor's task when using the above principle is to make explicit that which is currently implicit and help to 'state the obvious'. The aim is to facilitate the client's awareness of what is seen, heard and felt without offering interpretation or advice, which allows the counsellor's working hypothesis to be confirmed through direct experience.

Second, *gestalt identification and dialogue* is a technique which elucidates the meaning of the client's process, through the experience of identification. This involves the client experientially 'identifying with' an image, an aspect of herself, a dream component, a feeling or even another person, in order to evoke increased awareness of the topic at hand. The client's perception of another person is assumed to be largely a projection of her own unconscious aspects. The counsellor invites identification and a dialogue to occur between herself and identification with the other, as a means of working through the dynamics of the intrapersonal subjective relationship. The client can also identify and hold a dialogue with images, subpersonalities and symbols.

In the earlier example of the bear which represented the client's repressed power, the client was asked to identify with the bear in order to learn more of its essential nature. She was then invited to become herself again and to establish a dialogue (albeit subjective) between herself and the bear. This technique of identification brings into consciousness revelations which were previously unknown to the client and that are often surprising and unexpected. If addressing an interpersonal difficulty, the client can, through the process of identification, hold a dialogue with the person involved. This serves two functions: it develops empathetic understanding of the other as well as enabling the client to understand at a deeper level her own attitudes, feelings and behaviour and to re-own any projections.

Using gestalt in the above way has no contra-indications for the counselling of 'healthy neurotics'. Due to the principle of *organismic self-regulation*, adopted by Fritz Perls, the founder of gestalt therapy, a client will work only at a level and to a depth which is appropriate for her psyche. With emphasis being placed upon personal responsibility and choice, gestalt is an approach that can be fruitfully integrated within the context of psychosynthesis counselling.

We have looked at the levels of psychosynthesis counselling, the counsellor and the basic techniques she will use. It is time to turn our attention to the client and the beginning of the counselling work. The next chapter outlines the counselling work from the initial interview and diagnosis which prepares us for the first phase of counselling.

4

DIAGNOSIS AND ASSESSMENT

THE INITIAL INTERVIEW

When Caroline, whom we met earlier, walked into the counsellor's office and glanced nervously at the surroundings, the room seemed normal enough, with a light, quiet atmosphere. She noticed fresh flowers, pictures on the wall of stars and galaxies, a collection of ornamental stones and sea shells and, in the centre of the room, two armchairs facing each other. There was nothing very threatening here. She relaxed a little.

Caroline was in her mid-forties. She was thin and walked with stooped shoulders. Her face carried a look of despair, deeply etched by years of anxiety, countless failures and, more recently, separation from her husband followed by a divorce.

Life was so empty and meaningless that in recent months she had even contemplated suicide. Her feelings of loneliness and insecurity were punctuated with rage that her life was devoid of the slightest sense of fulfilment. She found herself unable to control her behaviour and had recently begun physically to abuse her two small children. Her perception of herself and her situation was that she was a helpless victim – both to her inner world with its intense emotional disruptions and to the outer world which she blamed for not providing her with the opportunities she needed to rebuild her life.

In short, her subjective experience of herself was that she was unloved, indeed unlovable, and that she was powerless to effect any constructive change. It was in this psychological state that she had decided to seek help. Emotional pain was the motivating factor; although she was convinced that the problems of her existence were not of her own creation, Caroline sought only the alleviation of that pain. She was unaware of the tacit promise that psychosynthesis counselling carries – a promise which would speak to the inherent tendency in her (and in us all) to:

- find our individuality and affirm that identity as unique;
- express ourselves as autonomous, independent beings;
- love and be loved;
- become the masters of our own lives.

More deeply it promises:

- to provide a sense of belonging to a larger whole, of being more than an isolated individual;
- unity and a sense of being one with self and others;
- to reveal meaning and purpose in life;
- a transcendence of individuality and existential identity;
- to answer a deep yearning for life's potential for beauty and goodness.

They sat down together. The counsellor was silent, waiting for Caroline to speak; she in turn was waiting for the counsellor to begin. In psychosynthesis counselling, the first principle of an initial interview is to confront the obvious. 'How do you feel about being here today, Caroline? Are you a little nervous?' Most potential clients respond affirmatively and it is useful to acknowledge that anxiety is a natural response to an unknown situation.

The next principle is to make explicit the purpose of the interview and to inform the potential client of what is going to happen in the next hour. The important factors are:

- to realize that this is a time for the counsellor and client to get to know each other;
- to hear what brings the client to seek counselling; her major presenting issues. Assessment and diagnosis begin with the initial interview;
- to elicit details of the client's biographical and existential life;
- to learn about the client's physical, emotional, mental and spiritual (transpersonal) life;

- to determine the appropriateness of this form of counselling;
- for the client to interview the counsellor to assess whether she is a person she feels she can trust.

It is important for the counsellor to know as much as possible about the client's background from the outset. The reasons for this are several: the counsellor must know any serious past or present medical conditions; have information about significant childhood traumas; obtain as broad a picture as possible of the context of the client's life. Without this ground of information it would be irresponsible to just *dive in* and start working.

After stating the purpose of the interview the counsellor will begin to gather basic information of age, marital status, family details and medical history. She will also pay attention to the potential client's general state of health as well as her subjective relationship to her body. She will ask a series of questions along the following lines: Have there been any serious illnesses as a child or adult? Does the client have a psychiatric background? Has she ever had treatment for psychological problems? How would she define her general state of health? Is she having or has she had any consistent medication in the past? Does the client consider herself to be strong or fragile, fit or unfit?

The counsellor will let the dialogue develop giving the client space for spontaneous self-expression, interjecting some of the following when appropriate. Areas for more factual questions are: Where did the client spend her childhood? How would she describe her background? What was her family life like? Was her father present throughout her childhood? What was his profession? And mother, did she work? Did the client have brothers and sisters? What is significant to her about her childhood?

Has the client previously done any psychological work or had treatment for mental problems? If she has done psychological work before, what was the outcome? Did she experience it as helpful? Did her life change as a result? Exploring this last aspect is essential, for it will provide the counsellor with important information. If the client has had many therapeutic experiences, tenacious resistance may exist. Previous successful counselling will provide a sound basis for more. If, however, it was not beneficial, negative transference could be carried over.

Difficult and confrontative aspects of the client's life are left until later in order to establish a rapport and to enable some degree of trust to be built. Then, hopefully, when the client feels safe enough to be more open and honest, she can disclose more of her true motivation. When the counsellor senses that the moment is ripe, which can happen at any time, she will begin to probe the emotional level, exploring both the client's general feeling life and her presenting issues. Areas to uncover are: What is her relationship to affective experience? How does she deal with her feelings? Does she tend to express them or to contain them? Were her parents free with emotions? What models did they provide? Gathering information on these factors provides the counsellor with a larger gestalt of the client, so important if the counsellor is to work on the transformation of underlying growth patterns rather than on symptom alleviation.

The counsellor might continue with: What role did the client play in her family? Was she a peacemaker, a rebel, a good girl or a clown, for example? This will help the counsellor to get a sense of the client's family system. Perhaps the most essential questions the counsellor needs to ask are the following: What are the client's greatest challenges in life? What is it that really brings her to counselling? What are her deepest concerns and how does she experience them? Have there been any significant turning points or crises in her life?

Throughout the interview the counsellor will actively listen and will mirror, reflect and paraphrase the client's communication. This helps to establish a relationship and shared language, and allows the client to experience being seen, heard and understood. The counsellor will also encourage her to ask questions if they arise during their dialogue.

Throughout the initial interview the counsellor will be monitoring *internally* her response to the potential client in terms of a complementary countertransference. The inner responses which the client evokes from the counsellor provide invaluable information on the needs and dynamics the client might present in counselling. It will alert the counsellor to the kind of *holding environment* she would be called upon to create for the client. It will show her potential areas of challenge for them both. Importantly, the counsellor's countertransference response will enable her to discriminate the degree of disturbance the client is living within. A counsellor found herself feeling aggressive towards a potential client in an initial interview. This alerted her to the reality that the client had been systematically abused. Another example is when the counsellor experienced a strong pull/demand to take care of the client which symbolized a helplessness and resistance to growing up. The client may in fact present herself as so needy that the counsellor is tempted to offer extra sessions at special times. Our tendency will be to react towards the client in the way that most significant others have done – this would not serve the client, but simply repeat other relationships from her past.

Psychosynthesis places emphasis upon well-being beyond the personality and its pathology. That which is meaningful and valuable to the client in her life is paramount. Information on and understanding of her spiritual life is extremely relevant. What makes her heart sing? Where in life does she experience the most fulfilment and joy? What gives her life meaning? What vision does she have of the future and how would she wish it to be? What are her strengths and positive qualities, even if they only exist in potential? Has she had moments of significance or peak experiences? Has she ever experienced a deeper sense of identity? What is the purpose of her life?

Exploring areas such as these can provide the counsellor with an enlarged perspective of the person. Within this context clients cease to be perceived as people who need to be fixed, helped or corrected. The counsellor's task goes beyond the relief of the symptoms, which tends only to modify behaviour rather than address the deeper levels of the client's reality, to promote a greater sense of well-being.

Finally, the interview may be concluded with any outstanding questions that the client may have. The counsellor will invite questions on the way she works, the psychosynthesis model of the human being and the methods and techniques she will use. As psychosynthesis counselling requires the active and willing participation of the client, these questions deserve attention. In addition, the client may also want to know about the counsellor's background and experience.

Obviously if the client is severely distressed or emotionally agitated at the outset of the initial interview, the counsellor will be sensitive to this. It may be necessary first to address her distress and restore some equilibrium. As soon as appropriate, however, the counsellor will ensure that she gathers knowledge of the client's background.

The counsellor will summarize the format of psychosynthesis counselling, its duration and contracted termination. Although the time of termination may change during the course of counselling, it is advisable to set boundaries rather than leave it open ended. Often a psychosynthesis counsellor will propose an initial contract of six sessions, to be reviewed and assessed before continuing. The counselling can be short- or long-term depending on the needs, preference and temperament of the client.

ESTABLISHING A WORKING HYPOTHESIS

At this point, counsellor and client have begun to establish a relationship and, hopefully, created a positive context upon which to build. Based upon her increased personal experience of the client, the counsellor is now in a position to reflect more extensively and create an overall working hypothesis. This working hypothesis applies to the macrocosm, the client's life as a whole, and to the microcosm, a particular presenting issue. It must be a loosely held vision which the counsellor can verify as the counselling progresses.

Whether the counsellor knows it or not, she will hold a particular perception of the client which, unless addressed, will remain unconscious. From her unconscious perception choices of how to work with the client are still made. Thereby the counsellor risks imposing her own judgements of normative health, losing sight of individual uniqueness and manipulating the client's psyche towards her unverified perception. Psychosynthesis suggests that it is both wise and practical for the working hypothesis to be consciously created, loosely held and eventually verified or adjusted.

Emerging Purpose

Assagioli suggested that in a healing relationship, one which fosters transformation and deeper well-being, the counsellor will maintain a 'bifocal vision' of the client. Bifocal vision involves perceiving the client from a dual perspective; first, as a Self, a being with a purpose in life and with immense potential for love, intelligence and creativity; and second, as a personality, an individual made up of a unique blend of physical, emotional and mental characteristics.

He further recommended that the counsellor look towards the Self and the superconscious when seeking the potential for change in the client's life, and towards the personality for the client's existential experience, motivation to work on herself and intention to change.

A sense of *emerging purpose* in psychosynthesis counselling is vital in each session, for it provides a progressive context within which the client can experience herself and make choices. The client will report many experiences which will prompt the counsellor to speculate: What is trying to emerge through these difficulties, and what potential for growth is contained within them? If the client was unconsciously seeking a step forward, what might it be? What old behaviour pattern is dying in order for something new to be born?

Emerging purpose is based on the idea that whatever is psychologically foreground for the client is not just fate or an accident. Meaning is attributed to the fact that a particular problem is foreground at a particular moment. Problems are seen to have hidden purpose which will advance the client in her development. Something new is trying to be born. Emerging purpose is the progressive step forward contained within the client's difficulty. It is held to be inherent within the client's superconscious (higher unconscious) and the counsellor's task is to remain sensitive to this progressive thrust and to listen to a level behind the presented content. This larger vision sustains the immediate work of releasing blocks and confronting neuroses.

Furthermore, purpose is constantly changing. It can be likened to a seed which does not suddenly become a flower but progresses through a series of developments. It is possible, however, to envision the flower that the seed will become, and to recognize the steps in between. Purpose is this unfoldment from seed to flower.

One client, plagued by a conflict between a mentally critical part of herself and another which was very soft and compassionate, learned to disidentify and see the value of each. Rather than being locked in conflict, she learned to have both her mind and her feelings more available in her everyday life. At this stage of counselling her emerging purpose was the integration of mind and feelings. Next came the exploration of self-expression. Subsequently she felt that in order to express herself fully both mentally and emotionally, she needed to take more responsibility for her life. Self-affirmation, therefore, became the next phase of her emerging purpose.

Purpose is not the ultimate truth but it represents a possible way to define the client's growth and to provide a constructive framework for it. The point here is that emerging purpose is intimately connected with the difficulties the client is experiencing. An essential aspect of the counselling work is the coherent relationship between the death of old forms (characteristics, behaviour patterns, psychological identities) and the birth of the new. If framed in an expansive context, the energy of conflict is inherently creative.

The following are some examples of the intimate connection between emerging purpose and existential experience. One client who approached life primarily through her mind rather than through her feelings sought counselling because of psychosomatic stomach problems. She was out of touch with her emotional life which obviously, for her own well-being, needed to become a conscious experience. She had suppressed her feelings for years, and now she had stomach problems. Why? For what purpose? What was trying to emerge here?

On investigation the counsellor heard that the client was contemplating a major career shift in a direction which would require more of her feeling life to be available. In fact this career change would demand the expression of her more altruistic tendencies. As she was not open to her feelings these qualities could not emerge, and the existing psychological system had to open up. She was forced to listen to the problem in her stomach and through this to learn to listen to her feelings. This led to her becoming aware of her capacity to love. This way of framing the client's psychological experience provides a different perspective from perceiving the stomach problem as something to be eliminated.

Another client was having problems in her relationship with her husband, was locked into confrontation with her boss at work, was paranoid in her relationships with colleagues and was frequently getting sick. Rather than deal with these various problems as isolated entities, the counsellor sought the underlying theme and deeper message being communicated. The counsellor's working hypothesis, which proved to be accurate, was that the client needed to own her personal power.

A businessman sought counselling to learn to relax and to relieve stress. The counsellor determined that the client was exceptionally attached to the material world, and that his life had lost meaning. Her working hypothesis was that buried within his desire to relax, he was really unconsciously searching for something worthwhile to live for.

A successful teacher of small children came to counselling because she wanted to begin to teach adults. Although she was enthusiastic about it, she was filled with anxiety and self-doubt of which she wanted to be free. She was emotionally identified and often dominated by her feelings. This made it difficult for her to choose steps forward and to organize her life. The counsellor surmised that beneath it all lay the need to disidentify from her feelings, to experience herself as separate from them and to develop a stronger sense of autonomy.

Shortly after the death of her father, a middle-aged woman sought counselling for depression and a recurring fear of cancer. She was aware that she needed to grieve over her loss but she could only feel her depression. Through counselling she discovered that her father's death had evoked her own fear of dying and, more importantly, some self-destructive tendencies. Emerging through this difficulty was a search for authenticity. She longed for her life to be more than it was. She knew that something was missing and that if she did not find it, she would *die*. By exploring her superconscious and finding qualities that were uniquely hers, the client discovered that what she really wanted to do and be in life was very different from what she had been taught. Her basic world view had not been her own. She chose to let go of her conditioned perspective towards life and to adopt one that reflected her inner stature.

Initial Motivation: Freedom from Pain

It is not, however, a sense of emerging purpose that draws clients to seek counselling. Nearly always it is the deep pain that they are experiencing, either connected to a particular problem or event, or of an existential nature. Pain in this context is one of the most powerful motivating forces for change. Although seemingly negative, this step provides a healthy energizing force for the beginning of counselling. 'It hurts.' 'I want to get better.' 'I am not getting what I want.' 'I want to be free.' 'I want to know what is happening to me.' The counsellor has to respond sensitively to whatever is motivating the client in the moment. Motivational energy can be defined as that which brings a client to present a problem and it is often related to seeking pleasure and avoiding pain. However, it usually reflects a deeper need, contained within the problem.

The counsellor can hear these desires of the client and respond to them while maintaining the bifocal vision which enables her to see that more is happening than is immediately obvious. The counsellor will keep her eyes open for signs of an implicit desire to go beyond the immediate motivation. This hidden urge towards a greater state of health than merely mending the pain constitutes a search for purpose and is a key component in the process of healing in psychosynthesis counselling.

The counsellor can both hypothesize an emerging purpose and listen to the immediate motivation. It is not something explicit but, when perceived with a broadened vision, the counsellor will reframe the client's experience, enabling the potential contained within the problem to be actualized.

Intention

In psychosynthesis counselling, the fostering of the client's motivation is seen as a progressive series of steps leading to a clear intention for change. The task of the counsellor is to evoke from the client a constructive awareness of what she really wants, which will tend to shift her from motivation to conscious intention. This shift is made through evoking the client's will, and often requires a shift from a negative orientation to a positive one. It involves the clarification of why she is presenting an issue, what she wants to have happen and where she wants to go. Thus, for example: 'I don't want to feel shy and nervous' to 'I want to be confident and strong.' 'I'm angry with my wife, she tries to control me all the time' to 'I want to honour what is right for me and be in a harmonious relationship with my wife.' 'I want to get rid of my inner critic' to 'I want to be more self-accepting.'

Sometimes a client will come to a counselling session with a positive intention for change already mobilized. She may have the psychological awareness or maturity to engage her intention. Others will be surprisingly vague and will need to clarify their direction. Intentionality implies a commitment from the client, an affirmation of concern for her existence and a determination to do something about it.

Like purpose, intention is vital to a counselling session, for it provides the strength for the client to move in spite of resistances and the discomfort and pain which may be encountered along the way. No change is effortless and often the client must live through painful disintegration prior to a step forward. This disintegration can be filled with uncertainty and paradox, so a dedicated intention to continue is vital to sustain her.

'How would you like this to change and be?' is a key question. If, for instance, the client presents an inability to communicate, it might be inspiring for her to know *how* she would like to communicate. Her intention to communicate in a specific way creates an ideal model, motivates and shifts her towards a constructive image and commitment to work. Shifting the immediate motivation to a conscious positive intention sets a recognizable goal for the client.

Another key question is 'What would you be like if you were free of this problem?' From the beginning a model is created of a direction for the counselling and again this evokes the client's will. Unless the client experiences that her intention is at the core of working through her difficulties, then the counsellor becomes the saviour rather than the client being a self-determining agent and the cause of her own growth. This subtle point is vitally important lest the counselling become the only forum for growth. If a client can experience that she chose the direction, goal and outcome, she is empowered to do so again outside the counselling arena.

Intention engages the client's personal will and choice to move in a certain direction. There is a qualitative difference between 'I want' (initial motivation) and 'I will' (conscious intention). This intentionality may be present without ever being made explicit. The counsellor may sense the client's will without evoking it to become conscious. The client who wills to learn to be intimate, for example, will have a much easier time dealing with her vulnerability and letting go of defences against intimacy than merely seeking to rid herself of vulnerability.

Evoking intention is a general principle by which the counsellor provides an opportunity for the client to co-operate with her emerging potential and to go beyond self-imposed limitations. It would be unproductive, however, for the counsellor to do this if the client were at that moment assessing herself from a limited perspective or partial identification. For example, a client who was identified with being very soft and loving (as a defence against the threat of rejection), and who allowed other people consistently to take advantage of her, presented her anger and assertive feelings as a problem to be eliminated. It was apparent to the counsellor that the client's aggressive feelings were actually an unconscious attempt of her psyche to balance itself. What was most appropriate was to elicit her potential to have the choice to assert herself, when appropriate, or to be loving. To evoke this client's intention would only have mobilized a distorted motivation and resistance to growth.

A client who was over-stressed presented the desire to be more strong and in control and to accomplish more in her life. The counsellor knew, however, that this person was working full time, pursuing an Open University degree, running a family of four and even studying during her lunch hours. To be more in control was not the real issue. She had structured her difficulty from a limited identity which valued achievement and did not allow her to acknowledge her personal needs. She was tired and burnt out. She needed, at a deeper level, to let go of overachieving and to include her personal needs. For the counsellor to have followed the client's initial request would only have fuelled her imbalance.

In cases such as these, it is wise for the counsellor to *wait* for the client's awareness to enlarge before eliciting her intention. If counsellor and client explore the difficulty, either verbally or experientially, a wider perspective will eventually emerge. The counsellor does not try to change the client's direction, but rather facilitates an expansion of consciousness to *get all the cards on the table* before establishing a direction. She does not want to reinforce a crystallized stance or a limited perception in the client.

Due to the compensatory function of the unconscious, the opposite will tend to try to come forth. If the client is identified with being very hard working, her desire for play will be knocking at the door; if she is always very self-sacrificing, her need for self-assertion is lurking nearby; if she appears only soft and sweet, a strong woman lives in her unconscious. It will reveal itself through body language, tone of voice, a comment made in passing or through insight.

Through fear or habit we try to suppress, consciously or unconsciously, this *opposite* force to our perceived self-image. It is the aim of the counsellor to encourage, help to develop and refine all aspects so that the client can eventually play the full keyboard of her personality rather than only a few notes.

SUMMARY

The client comes to the counselling session with a presenting issue and a particular motivation. The counsellor helps to formulate, clarify and define the issue while broadening the client's awareness. The client develops in herself a positive intention for the direction of the work. The work begins. In psychosynthesis counselling the model of emerging purpose and motivation, shifting to intention, is used in the overall assessment phase and should be applied to each presenting problem in the client's life.

Plan

Not every gesture of a counsellor is necessarily spontaneous. There needs to be some degree of forethought, some conscious attention to the overall direction of the counselling work. In psychosynthesis counselling, planning is seen as an essential function involving the client's active participation. The counsellor and client will together create a sense of the larger direction in which the client wishes to go.

The plan consists of a model or description of the client's presenting issues and existential experience. It creates an overall assessment of problem areas to be addressed and a loosely held strategy for working. The plan is based on past experiences with the client, on intuitive perception and on a rational formulation of what would be the most useful way to work.

It includes the counsellor's diagnosis of the total situation, her working hypothesis on emerging purpose and bridging that with the client's intention. Although the counsellor may not make explicit her overall perception of the plan, she will tend to share with the client the surmised next steps. The plan always requires inclusion and respect for the client's expressed preferences and choices.

The plan can take a pragmatic and practical form. What exactly does the client want to work on and in what sequence? What is most essential to address first? The strategy for working may include several methods from which the client can choose. The plan includes the moment-to-moment choice of interventions that the counsellor makes based upon her working hypothesis, upon the client's responses and experience, and upon what seems to be emerging. Consequently the plan may change during the course of a session as more information emerges, as the client wills and as the counsellor adjusts both her perception and interventions. If the plan is off-target or premature, the counsellor must be flexible enough to adjust or let go of it. However, as the counsellor's unconscious will always have a plan or a strategy for working, it is wiser to make it explicit to herself rather than allow it to remain implicit.

The function of a plan serves a dual purpose: it provides a potential map or model of the ideal sequence for the work and it continues to evoke the client's intention to invest herself fully in it. Planning is, however, not a static process. It may undergo dynamic changes as the counselling progresses and consequently will need to be reviewed regularly.

The plan is a blueprint for actualizing the client's *ideal model*: where the client wants to go as defined by her own experience and perception of herself. It can foster a clear realization of the task at hand. Assagioli (1965: 26) noted that some clients have a clear and distinct picture of their aim from the outset which is useful for planning. He writes:

> This picture should be realistic and authentic, that is, in line with the natural development of the given individual and therefore capable – at least in some measure – of realisation and should not be a neurotic, unreal 'idealized' image. A genuine ideal model has a dynamic creative power; it facilitates the task by eliminating uncertainties and mistakes; it concentrates the energies.

It is this ideal model which will determine the content and details of the plan, which leads to the initial phase of counselling.

5

THE INITIAL PHASE OF COUNSELLING

Following the initial interview and the formation of the counsellor's early working hypothesis, the main body of work begins. Although the length of counselling is determined by the client's stated desire and the nature of her presenting issues, the first phase of psychosynthesis counselling typically comprises between fifteen and twenty sessions. It should be noted, however, that psychosynthesis also lends itself well to short or brief therapy, which can typically vary from six to thirty sessions. In this chapter we will look at this initial phase, in particular considering the counsellor's aim and intention, the issues most commonly presented by the client and the counsellor's approach in addressing these issues.

THE FIRST SESSION

The Counsellor's Aim

In psychosynthesis, the counsellor's aim for the first session is twofold: first, to continue to establish the interpersonal relationship and build trust and, second, to stimulate the client's choice to move forward in a progressive direction.

Establishing the relationship As mentioned in Chapter 2, the psychosynthesis counsellor has the intention of providing the client, for a time, an *external unifying centre* as a means of psychological *mirroring* which creates an empathic relationship with the significant other of the counsellor. An empathic relationship enables what Winnicott (1987) called a nurturing or facilitating environment. It also provides for the client the positive *recognition* that was missing in relationships with early caregivers and enables her knowing of personal selfhood. The creation of this empathic context will imbue the on-going environment within which counsellor and client build trust.

The counsellor knows that without trust, authentic communication is greatly inhibited; nor will the client feel secure enough to disclose her deepest feelings. Essentially, the more disturbed the client, the more time is required to build trust, and for most clients this is not something that happens in one session. Consequently it is an aim that the counsellor holds throughout the first phase of counselling.

From the beginning the tendency for the client to transfer childhood relationships, usually parental, on to her relationship with the counsellor is present. Authority transference is more likely at this vulnerable moment for the client. The counsellor will stay alert to both her subjective experience of the client and behavioural clues to this happening. There is not much she can do about it at this stage but remain sensitive to the client.

The counsellor will work to build trust and establish a therapeutic alliance primarily through the *quality* of her presence. The most effective tool that the counsellor has is her ability to hold an expanded context of *bifocal vision*, in which she perceives the client as a *Being* who has a purpose in life and challenges and obstacles to meet in order to fulfil that purpose. The counsellor will actively maintain the attitude that this client is unique, with her own creative potential and capacity to create meaning in her life. She trusts that the client ultimately has all the answers needed within, and her task is to evoke this inner knowing. In this way the counsellor validates the client's human integrity and perceives her as more than just a problem to be solved.

The counsellor will indicate her acceptance of the client through active listening, paraphrasing and reflecting the client's communications; and most importantly, by letting her know that her experiences are valid. Furthermore she will show interest in the details of the client's life, not taking for granted the content of her presenting issues. She will ask questions that expand the client's understanding of her issues so that the client feels her care and concern, without labelling, judging or interpreting.

Stimulating the client's choice to grow   In psychosynthesis the will is the central function of the Self, coming from the core of human experience and essential to psychospiritual health. Consequently, a psychosynthesis counsellor places the will at the centre of counselling and positively values it as an inner subjective experience necessary from the beginning. The counsellor will aim to evoke the client's will to be healed or, indeed, to heal herself. If it is lacking or overpowered by self-destructive tendencies, the counsellor's first interventions will be geared towards its arousal and strengthening.

Although obvious, this goal can easily become lost, especially if counsellor and client focus excessively on experiential work rather than on the final objective. Without the will, extensive exploration of her presenting problems can lead to an accentuation of their causes and, rather than being healed, the client simply develops a thorough knowledge of early childhood neuroses. Counselling then becomes a regressive and imprisoning circle which easily leads to a therapy-induced neurosis and, by the end of counselling, a client who is fully aware of, but identified with, her pathology.

The counsellor helps the client to envisage reaching a successful outcome to their work. She will ask questions like: What direction do you want to take? What do you really want to achieve from counselling? How would you be different than you are right now? What is most important to you to work on? Even if the client can vaguely glimpse the answers to these questions, they arouse the part of her that *wills* to be whole, to take responsibility for her life, to experience herself as a person who can act, rather than just react. The counsellor empowers the client to define her own strategy and plan for the counselling work.

How does the counsellor facilitate the client's vision of a positive path forward? The counsellor will initiate the exploration through active dialogue; however, if appropriate, she may suggest experiential work. Guided imagery can provide a structure through which the client can discover her immediate next step. Ideal model work can evoke a broader and longer-term vision of what is possible. A provocative question from the counsellor, like 'How would you like your life to be?', can inspire the client to set a positive goal.

A positive path forward is often accompanied by the counsellor addressing the client's pain. When people first begin counselling, emotional pain is primarily the driving force. Through empathic understanding the counsellor will encourage the client to share, and hopefully release, painful feelings which are in the foreground of her experience and need attention. By doing this, she communicates to the client that her pain is important, and continues to build their relationship.

The counsellor will also aim to communicate to the client that she is more than her pathology and show her that she can lead the direction of the work rather than have it prescribed for her. If the counsellor sees the client's healing solely in terms of the elimination of symptoms, it can induce in her a void which may be filled with other symptoms of similar strength. However, when the counsellor helps the client to find a positive purpose to which to aspire, the consciousness which underlies the symptoms can be transformed and more than just adaptive behavioural change occurs.

In the previous case of Caroline, the evocation of her will took several sessions before she dared to create a positive image of her life. With the counsellor's patient support and probing, however, she recognized that within all her pain there was a constructive element that brought her to counselling. She acknowledged that she had occasionally heard a small voice whispering to her that life could be more. The counsellor saw this statement as an opportunity to evoke from Caroline a positive impulse. She invited her to elaborate this small voice and listen to its message. Caroline reported that it was as if there was someone inside her who had the will to reach out and who wanted to discover the meaning which her life lacked.

Throughout the counselling the counsellor would regularly suggest that Caroline tune into and listen to the message of the 'small voice', which eventually led to Caroline herself playing the role of her *inner guide/wisdom* who was able to provide her with ways out of her endless struggle. This tuning in and listening to was brought about through the technique of guided imagery. The counsellor would invite Caroline to allow a symbolic image to appear for the small voice and to have an inner dialogue with it.

A psychosynthesis counsellor does not interpret the symbolic meaning of the client's images but through dialogue and gestalt identification encourages the client to do so. For example, one client's guiding image was a mountain path. Her interpretation of this was that a lot of hard work lay ahead but she had a clear path to follow which was definitely going somewhere. The counsellor asked her to visualize the top of her mountain and she discovered a clearing where many people were meeting. Her further interpretation was that although her life until then had been quite isolated, its direction was towards meaningful interaction with others. In moments when the counselling became arduous, the counsellor would ask her to evoke her mountain summit as a reminder of her ultimate goal.

A male client, a former drug addict, sought psychosynthesis counselling for difficulties with interpersonal relationships. He described his struggle with drug addiction and how, in order to free himself, he had built an extreme 'tough-guy' identity. The counsellor asked him how he would like to be at the end of counselling and to his surprise he heard himself saying that his goal was to become more soft and loving. In some ways this image horrified him yet he also cried at the glimpse of its possibility. The counsellor had evoked from within him a 'north star', as he called it, by which to guide himself.

The counsellor's goal is to help the client ascribe a positive meaning to the counselling and to see that its constructive unfoldment can grant reality to that meaning. This corresponds with what Viktor Frankl (1970) called the 'will to meaning' which takes the form of the acceptance of life and an act of faith in life itself. The counsellor helps the client to make an *act of will*, which enables her to approach counselling constructively.

If the client is, however, in an intense crisis or overwhelmed by negative psychological content, pain may be a primary motivator and it may be difficult or even inappropriate to generate further motivation. The counsellor will wait to motivate the client later at a more opportune moment through utilizing her inherent thrust for health. In some cases the client may not succeed in finding meaning or value in a forward direction. This reflects an inability to find meaning in life in general and alerts the counsellor to the depth of her difficulties.

AFTER THE FIRST SESSION

Defining the Presenting Problems

During the initial phase the client will present a host of difficulties which the counsellor must conceptualize in a coherent way in order to proceed with the work. Although psychosynthesis avoids normative definitions of health and step-by-step recipes for the client, the counsellor is likely to follow this sequence:

1   She will invite the client to elaborate on her current conflicts, on her problems and on what she feels are the major obstacles to leading a fulfilling life. In this exploration the counsellor will focus the client's

attention on her problematic behaviour and on what changes she would like to make. While doing this the counsellor will rationally and intuitively assess which methods and techniques of psychosynthesis would be best for addressing the client's problems.

2   Through further dialogue and discussion with the client, the counsellor will refine her working hypothesis. She will then put the strategy defined in Chapter 4, 'Establishing a working hypothesis' (see p. 69), into action and choose the appropriate technique according to the client's temperament and readiness for experiential work.

In the initial phase, counselling focuses most frequently on the following areas:

1   chronic life patterns;
2   subpersonality conflicts and limited identities;
3   self-identification and psychological freedom.

CHRONIC LIFE PATTERNS

Definition of Chronic Life Patterns

Experiences which are familiar and repetitious are often found in the client's presenting problems. It is as if some uncontrollable force is in operation, conditioning both inner and outer experience. Recurring situations, seemingly outside of the client's control, result in predictable and limited behavioural responses. Caroline's life was pervaded by feelings of impotency and inadequacy and she unconsciously believed herself to be a helpless victim of unfortunate life circumstances. Again and again her experience seemed to confirm this reality and she felt hopeless to effect any positive change.

Caroline's behaviour was beyond her control and she could not choose to be otherwise, insisting that *life had done it to her*. With the passage of time these limiting behaviours became increasingly painful and dysfunctional.

Every chronic life pattern has its historical base, its biography, often traumatic, around which many other painful experiences accumulate. Whether positive or negative, the core experience tends to repeat itself again and again, forming a generalized behaviour pattern which in similar situations evokes similar responses. Eventually the client will perceive her whole world through this 'psychological system' and it will colour vividly her attitudes and expectations (see also Grof, 1979).

The memories belonging to such a life pattern will have a similar basic theme and carry a strong emotional charge of the same quality. For example, a pattern of low self-esteem will contain the client's memories of past experiences, of the humiliating and degrading situations that damaged it. A system of impotency and lack of healthy self-assertion will carry memories of moments where the client was victimized. There will be defence mechanisms, compensations and even physical symptoms.

Strategy for Working with Chronic Life Patterns

The psychosynthesis counsellor's strategy for working through tenacious and dysfunctional patterns involves addressing them on three complementary levels: experience, understanding and transformation. The somatic and affective aspects of a problem must be experienced; mental understanding is essential as well as healing in a positive direction, which includes a developmental step forward being taken by the client.

Experiencing the pattern   In addition to active dialogue the counsellor will encourage the client to enter into the physical and emotional experience of her difficulties. Using the tool of guided imagery she may invite the client imaginatively to relive, vividly and with great detail, the most recent time she felt the problem. This 'reliving' tends to evoke the same old emotions and physical sensations, brings the pattern into conscious experience and often produces a cathartic release. The counsellor would continue by directing the client to relive an earlier time when she experienced the same difficulty, even if the circumstances were somewhat different.

The counsellor may guide this process of reliving the problem several times, frequently going back to early childhood. Emotional expression has the benefit of releasing repressed feelings and the counsellor aims for the client to relive the pattern experientially. This release is almost always liberating, and from a freer psychological state the client will gain an expansion in awareness.

Caroline's primary chronic pattern was one of being a victim and she was able to relive many experiences in this role. The earliest one was in childhood when she had been emotionally abused by her mother, who was a tough disciplinarian and had punished her for the slightest mistake. Caroline's victim experience was further perpetuated by a strict religious educational system which demanded acquiescence and servitude. She eventually began to perceive the world as a tyrannizing place. This perception was projected on to the environment resulting in it being re-created again and again.

Through the experience of imaginatively reliving the pattern and its accompanying catharsis, the counsellor helped Caroline to release the years of repressed anger which lay beneath her victim consciousness and to reclaim her self-respect. Her major defence mechanism, passive aggression, slowly gave way to learning to say no and to setting boundaries. The counsellor used gestalt dialogue to help her to release the introjected mother persecutor living within her, which eventually freed her capacity to love. The counsellor used the technique of grounding to bring these changes into Caroline's everyday life. This work required many sessions to come to fruition.

Understanding the pattern   Experience in itself is not enough fully to heal and transform a dysfunctional behaviour pattern. It must be blended with understanding. In order for the client to free herself from the control of the pattern, the counsellor needs to help her define and articulate her psychological system, its causes and developments, and make the connection with how it affects her life today. The counsellor's goal is to help the client to accept herself as she discovers how these experiences have coloured her consciousness and her self-image.

With Caroline, for example, although the counsellor helped her work through the negative experience that contributed to the creation and maintenance of her victim pattern, this in itself did not resolve the problem. In order to be fully transformed, Caroline's experience first needed to be examined in the light of insight and understanding. To resolve an issue thoroughly, the counsellor must help the client to grasp the abstraction behind the problem, and with this broader understanding comes the possibility of expanded choice.

Transformation of the pattern   Transformation implies evolution from a negative symptom to a positive outcome which provides a qualitative leap to a more profound change. Transforming a negative psychological pattern involves more than merely eliminating dysfunctional behaviour; it requires the client to take a step forward which is both developmentally progressive and which fosters realization of a potential for positive change contained within the problem. The counsellor will aim to have the client discover this implicit creative possibility.

This level of changing a chronic behaviour pattern involves actively redirecting the emotional energy that is bound up in the old pattern into healthier modes. The counsellor uses the techniques of grounding and creative expression as a means of translating the insights gained through experience and understanding into action and behavioural change. The counsellor's strategy was for Caroline, in her everyday life, to move beyond being a victim by helping her to explore new behaviours. Caroline learned to say 'no' and to set boundaries, something she was previously unable to do. She also chose to begin to initiate friendships and transform her pattern of projecting tyranny on to the environment.

The counsellor will use the safety of the counselling session as a place to *try out* new behaviours. For example, when Caroline was learning to say 'no', the counsellor would offer alternative ways in which they could work and techniques to use, in order for her to learn to make choices. As Caroline was increasingly able to do so, the counsellor also provided her with choices requiring self-assertion and self-direction. Caroline had previously been unable to maintain eye contact for more than a few seconds. The counsellor asked her to try out holding eye contact a bit longer and to report when it became uncomfortable. Each time Caroline broke eye contact, they examined the obstacle and the counsellor encouraged her to choose to let go of it. In this way the counsellor used their relationship to encourage Caroline to find new ways of relating.

If the client is working with a new communication skill such as expressing her feelings, the counsellor will offer her opportunities to do so within the session. In addition, the counsellor would use ideal-model work to enable the client to visualize doing what previously felt impossible. Once the client can *imagine* herself taking a step, it becomes much more possible to do so in everyday life. These operations all contribute to replacing dysfunctional behaviours with healthy ones.

SUBPERSONALITY CONFLICTS AND LIMITED IDENTITIES

Definition of Subpersonalities

Paul was the ex-drug addict mentioned earlier, who had developed a capable and assertive persona in order to overcome his addiction. Many years ago, while facing the agony of drug withdrawal and coping with rehabilitation, he had learned to be strong, determined and autonomous. At a certain point, however, his hard independence became problematic and no longer served him. He discovered another part of himself that longed to be intimate but felt inadequate. This part of him believed that he would be rejected and deeply hurt if he opened up to others. When the opportunity for intimacy presented itself, he was overcome with shyness and reverted to his 'tough guy', who needed no one. It was as if two different people lived within him.

Louise was a rebellious feminist who was outspoken and intolerant of others. She fought for the plight of the down-trodden with an explosive ferocity. She often rowed with authority figures and found it difficult to sustain employment. When with her parents, however, Louise was a model of conforming behaviour and always gave in to their wishes. Her self-image when conforming was one of being a 'good girl'; diametrically opposed to the feminist 'crusader'. Yet another side of Louise greatly appreciated beauty: she frequently visited places of nature and maintained a mystical belief in the divinity of all life.

What do Louise and Paul have in common? Both of them seemingly had more than one personality which they occupied apparently randomly. Both were unconscious of their intermittent identification with particular ways of being, behaving and perceiving the world. They became lost in habitual states of consciousness which determined their experience and which occurred as a reaction to the environment. They had no internal reference point or centre of identity underlying their several personalities and were therefore prisoners of their psyches.

Subpersonalities are autonomous configurations within the personality as a whole. They are psychological identities, coexisting as a multitude of lives within one person; each with its own specific behaviour pattern, and corresponding self-image, body posture. feelings and beliefs. Their unique characteristics form a relatively unified whole.

Each subpersonality has an exclusive way of responding. We are often different when we are with our children compared to when we are in our workplace; or in certain challenging situations we quickly lose the calm self-assured demeanour that we display most of the time. When we shift our identifications in this way it is often in reaction to the demands of the situation. If we are lucky, we are drawn into the subpersonality that is *suitable* and can act appropriately for the circumstances. More often, however, we are unaware of the expectations from the environment and the demands of our inner world that control us. We are caught in ambivalence, confusion or conflict.

Being identified with a subpersonality is often unconscious and largely beyond our control. Our identification will change in a response to the demands of both inner and outer conditions, much more than to our desire and will. Most of the time the ex-addict client had little choice but to be a tough guy and the feminist was, in many situations, unable to do anything other than rebel.

Subpersonalities, like those mentioned above, develop as a means of meeting some basic need. Paul's tough guy fulfilled his need to be strong and independent, yet he also had a part who needed to love; Louise's feminist had a need for self-assertion but her good girl needed approval. These needs are basic to human experience and in themselves not problematic. Only through over-identification do they become a tyranny as this also excludes other sides of our personality.

What does it mean to be prisoner of a subpersonality? If we are identified with any one subpersonality, we experience that we *are* that subpersonality. Only this subpersonality's attitude is available. Its behaviour is compulsive, its view is narrow-minded and its feelings are limited. We need access to our entire personality if we are to be able to choose alternative and appropriate behaviours. The counsellor's aim, when working with negative life issues using the subpersonality model, is to free the client from the dominating and limiting behaviour that a subpersonality may cause.

Strategy for Working with Subpersonalities

In the early stages of counselling it is common for the client to experience a confusing and upsetting multiplicity in her personality. The *many voices* in our head all talking at once is a classic example. Rather than being one coherent being, we seem to be a more or less integrated conglomeration of many people. Other systems of psychology recognize that there are divisions within the personality: Freud's ego, id, superego (Freud, 1936); Jung's animus/anima or unconscious persona and shadow (Jung, 1933); Perls' (1970) topdog/underdog; Berne's adult, parent, child (Harris, 1973); Assagioli's subpersonalities (Assagioli, 1965: 74). These systems all indicate the recognition that the personality is not one subject. Assagioli's model of subpersonalities elaborated and described the richness, variety and multiplicity of the personality.

The psychosynthesis counsellor will use the subpersonality model as a strategy for addressing multiplicity, limited identifications and conflicting elements in the client. The client may feel confused by her own inconsistent behaviour and seeming inability to control herself The counsellor will aim to increase the client's perception of her own multiplicity by helping her discover how often she modifies her outlook, how her self-image regularly changes, how her perception of others varies and how inconsistent is her behaviour. As the client presents her life situation, the counsellor will use the subpersonality model to help clarify and order her difficulties.

Psychosynthesis offers several techniques for working with subpersonalities based on the principles of recognition, acceptance and integration.

Recognition of subpersonalities   Through dialogue with the client, it may become evident to the counsellor that an unconscious identification is preventing her from resolving the presenting issue. Often the client's existential situation indicates which subpersonalities need attention at any one time. As it is not advisable to work with too many subpersonalities, the counsellor will aim to help the client recognize those that seem more central or more important. Becoming aware of a subpersonality is the first step towards freedom from its limitations and distortions.

The early development of a subpersonality, its struggle to fulfil its needs and to express itself, usually occurs outside conscious awareness. Often an individual becomes aware of the situation only after some years of a subpersonality's development and in many cases only when the identification has become problematic. The counsellor's intention is to increase the client's recognition of the role of the *players* in her difficulties, for the purpose of initiating the process of change.

Once the principle of identification is understood, it is usually quite easy for the client to recognize relevant subpersonalities corresponding to her inner experience, and all that is needed to identify them is the counsellor's encouragement simply to look for them. There are several ways of doing this. First, following the counsellor's brief explanation of the subpersonality model, with active dialogue and assessment of the material that emerges in the therapy situation, the client can be guided to formulate and define a subpersonality or subpersonalities. Once defined, the counsellor might invite the client to close her eyes and allow a symbolic image for the subpersonality to emerge. This will tend to expand her awareness and deepen her ability to recognize the subpersonality.

Another method is for the counsellor to initiate a structured exercise as an evocative means of recognition. This method is valuable not only for recognizing subpersonalities, but also for understanding their behaviour patterns and interaction, and for harmonizing them. Two exercises commonly used in psychosynthesis counselling for subpersonality recognition are the Door exercise and the Evening Review.

The Door exercise is a mental-imagery technique where the client is instructed to visualize a door with the word *subpersonalities* written on it and to imagine that the subpersonalities that are important to her right now live behind it. She is then invited to open the door and let one or two subpersonalities come out and simply observe them without getting involved. If appropriate, the client can be encouraged to have a dialogue with a subpersonality in order to get to know it better.

The Evening Review is a grounding technique for increasing awareness and recognition of subpersonalities which the client does at home, just before retiring at night. She is instructed to find a quiet place, free from outer distractions, and quietly and alertly to review her day in her mind, playing it like a movie but in reverse. If she has been working with a particular subpersonality, for instance the inner critic, she is encouraged to review her day, noticing moments when the critic was operating. This enables the client to become conscious of previously unconscious identifications and patterns of behaviour. While doing this she is encouraged to maintain the attitude of an objective observer.

As a third alternative for subpersonality recognition, mental-imagery techniques are remarkably effective and can be used extensively for both recognition of and therapeutic work with subpersonalities, especially when there is an unconscious identification. There are many 'guided daydreams' that deal primarily with subpersonalities and their interactions. In these the client is guided to a symbolic environment and invited to allow images of certain affective states or experiences to emerge and take on a symbolic form. In the course of the guided day-dream, dialogue and interaction may also occur between the client and her subpersonality in order to deepen her experience.

In imagery work, for example, the client may visit a meadow where she finds a cottage in which lives a subpersonality or subpersonalities relevant to her life situation. She can invite it (them) to come out of the cottage to make contact with her. If recognition is the primary goal, the imagery may stop there or it could be continued for further exploration. One client who was suffering from anxiety attacks discovered a child subpersonality chained up inside the cottage in the meadow. Accompanying this discovery was the recognition that this part of her was repressed in childhood, prevented from developing and consequently felt unable to cope with adult life. This recognition led to a period of therapeutic work with the 'frightened child' and its integration. (For a more detailed explanation of mental imagery work see Chapter 3, p. 54).

Mental imagery may also be used more directly for recognition of subpersonalities through guiding the client affectively into a current problem and inviting her to evoke symbolic images for the aspects of her which are connected with the problem. For example, with this technique an alcoholic client visualized the part of her who drank as an 'old, tired bag lady' who was lost and depressed, and lacked purpose in life. Another client with a repeating pattern of broken relationships found a part of herself that was desperately dependent, seeking to get her needs met and would drive others away by her clinging behaviour. Also living within her was one who despised this 'clinger', was angry and pushed away intimacy.

It must be noted that the above techniques often evolve the client beyond the recognition stage of subpersonality work, and that they can also further acceptance and integration.

Acceptance of subpersonalities   The client must first *accept* that negative aspects are there in order to begin the process of change and eventually to integrate a subpersonality within the personality as a whole. Unconsciously we tend to believe that accepting a subpersonality means it remaining forever as it is. In reality exactly the opposite is true. Rejecting a subpersonality creates a psychological block which stunts its growth and causes it to develop in a one-sided distorted fashion increasingly at odds with the rest of the personality. Its useful qualities, its skills, its strengths are not available. Once a subpersonality is accepted, however, its real needs may be discovered and fulfilled in healthier ways; its positive qualities enhanced and its negative ones dissipated. When we first recognize new subpersonalities, our attitude towards each of them. as towards people, can vary according to our values and our self-image. Generally we tend to accept a subpersonality that, according to our value system, we consider good and useful, while rejecting those perceived as bad, harmful or useless. Those consistent with our self-image are easily accepted and those that do not fit are usually rejected.

Acceptance of a subpersonality makes it possible for it to evolve and offers the only hope of transformation. Conflicting elements which are unconsciously repressed or consciously suppressed do not disappear. Their energy accumulates in the unconscious and will tend indirectly to present itself through dreams, fantasies, somatized symptoms, neurotic manifestations and irrational behaviour. Accepting a subpersonality provides space for development and differentiation.

On the surface all seemed fine but Anne was suffering from debilitating anxiety attacks. She had a successful career, healthy and bright children and a life full of meaningful activities. Her anxiety began when she was offered promotion at work which required her to manage a large staff. The counsellor observed that when Anne spoke of her anxiety her voice became whining; her lowered head and questioning eyes gave her the appearance of having regressed. She seemed to adopt an attitude of obedience laced with hidden resentment.

Following Anne's cues, the counsellor invited her to explore this behaviour by mirroring what she observed and by asking her how old she 'felt'. Anne replied that she felt about fourteen years old, and then recalled experiencing these feelings, which she thought she had conquered, in early adolescence. The counsellor then asked her to close her eyes and visualize the adolescent that she was unconsciously showing. This led to fruitful work with Anne's adolescent 'achiever' subpersonality who was desperate to perform well and be successful and represented Anne's unfulfilled love needs. Consequently on the surface Anne appeared to be secure and successful, while underneath she was driven by insecurity which invariably would be followed by self-criticism.

Although usually unconscious, subpersonalities can polarize in reaction to each other, often resulting in inner conflict. The counsellor must address each polarity before the conflict can be resolved. Suppression of the weaker subpersonality by the stronger one never works and will only cause more dissonance. The counsellor intuited that there must be another subpersonality who was driving Anne's achiever. She initiated guided imagery work with the intention of helping Anne to discover what lay beneath the achiever. When asked to close her eyes and find herself in a meadow with the achiever, Anne found her achiever's constant companion, a 'ruthless critic', who had great disdain for imperfection. The critic was hiding in a cave assessing Anne's imperfections and plotting to change her.

To the critic, imperfection equalled unlovableness. Anne's critic had worked for years trying to force this insecure achiever to be strong, unafraid and flawless. Although unsuccessful, this effort caused Anne to repress the achiever's insecurity and to follow the critic's guidance unfailingly. The counsellor invited Anne to reflect on how this critic limited her and she saw that the critic was a hard task master, relentlessly driving her forward and constantly making her feel inadequate.

Integration of subpersonalities The strategy of integrating subpersonalities into the personality as a whole is paramount. It is necessary to relieve fragmentation and to resolve inner conflicts. Integrating the parts into the larger whole promotes psychological healing and expands the client's inner resources for experience and self-expression. It releases repressed and blocked life-energy, increasing aliveness and well-being.

Not only must a subpersonality be integrated within the personality as a whole but, as we have seen, the relationship *between* subpersonalities is sometimes problematic. Each part must find its place and activity. Vargiu (1974: 84) stated:

> the process of integration leads from a general state of isolation, conflict, competition and repression of the weaker elements by the stronger ones to a state of harmonious cooperation in which the effectiveness of the personality is greatly enhanced, and its emerging aspects find the space and nourishment they need to develop fully.

In the earlier example, the counsellor's goal was to have Anne realize that it was her inner critic who did not like the achiever, not Anne herself. When Anne discovered this, she would be able to distance herself from both the critic and the achiever and accept her feelings of anxiety. In doing so she would effectively *disidentify* from the unconscious identification with this critic. The process would also foster Anne's awareness that ultimately she was not the achiever either.

The counsellor then used gestalt dialogue to enable Anne to get to know the critic and the adolescent and to build their relationship with the intention of Anne eventually integrating both as valid parts of her personality. This dialogue took place through using two chairs, one representing the critic, the other the achiever. The counsellor asked Anne to take first the critic's chair and as she did so to identify with the critic, imagining that she had become her. From this identification the counsellor invited the critic to speak to the anxious achiever, expressing her feelings towards her. A vicious attack followed with the critic telling the achiever all that was wrong with her. The counsellor then asked the client to move to the achiever's chair and respond to the critic's admonitions. Tears and childlike despair immediately erupted from the insecure achiever.

Through switching back and forth between the two chairs, the counsellor encouraged the client to let this dialogue and expression of feelings develop. The establishment and improvement of this relationship between subpersonalities is essential for their integration and the counsellor may spend many sessions with this type of experiential interaction. Her goal is for the client eventually to experience the core of a subpersonality in order to uncover its essential nature.

When the counsellor guides the client to move towards the core of a subpersonality, she inevitably finds some basic urge or need which is good. For practical purposes the counsellor operates with this principle in mind. No matter how many layers of distortion surround it, the basic need, the essential motivation, is a good one. The subpersonality has become dysfunctional due to repression and its inability to express itself directly. The real core of a subpersonality, not what it wants but what it needs, is positive. For example, the achiever needed love; the critic needed the security of being in control.

Deeper still, beneath a subpersonality's superficial behaviour lives a higher potential, some quality that it has to express. Subpersonalities are like people. If we treat them with compassion and understanding, they open up and give us the best of what they truly are. The counsellor creates opportunities for the client to delve deeper into a subpersonality in search of its potential contribution. For example, even Caroline's victim, discussed earlier, could eventually bring a positive contribution such as understanding and empathy for the suffering of others.

Any content of the psyche can become distorted. Compassion can become pity; love can become dependency; humour can become sarcasm; strength can become rigidity. But the converse is also true, for these qualities can be elevated to or transformed into their essential nature. The counsellor will help the client find a subpersonality's hidden potential. By using guided imagery to heal her childhood wounds, Anne discovered that her achiever contained her potential for sensitivity and compassion.

On the other hand, Anne's critic, once freed from the hidden purpose of trying to make the achiever perfect (and keeping her vulnerability hidden from the world), began to provide the useful quality of discrimination. This transformation occurred by the counsellor using the technique of disidentification. Once Anne disidentified from her critic and created psychological distance, she began to see what it actually had to offer. This process is described in the following section.

To find the answer to what a subpersonality ultimately has to offer, the counsellor will ask: at its core, what quality does this identity have? What quality lies behind its negative or distorted behaviour? Even a problematic subpersonality can eventually bring a positive contribution. The ex-addict's tough guy carried his potential for courage and perseverance. The feminist offered concern for the less fortunate and an alternative vision. Finding the qualities living at the heart of a subpersonality is possible only after a substantial amount of work has been done and is a longer-term aim of the counsellor.

Techniques used for subpersonality work   Techniques used for integrating subpersonalities are many and are often used in conjunction with each other to facilitate the client's work more effectively. Recognition, acceptance and integration are not linear strategies applied one after the other; rather, they are cyclical and interactive. The counsellor will mainly use experiential techniques to integrate unconscious content with what is known.

Mental imagery   may be used for the integration of subpersonalities in several ways. First, it can be used to evoke from the unconscious that which lies beneath the surface behaviour and to enlarge the client's awareness. The mental-imagery work described in the strategy of recognition will often be elaborated to include interaction between the client and her subpersonality or between two subpersonalities. With a more extended interaction the counsellor will guide the client to see deeper into a sub-personality's pattern of behaviour, its underlying needs, its *raison d'être* and its potential for change.

As an important part of this process, the counsellor will direct the client to *identify with* and become the subpersonality, thereby experiencing it from the *inside* and affectively knowing its reality. Much insight, often unexpected, comes from this imagery work. After such work the client may feel very differently towards a subpersonality. This often is the case when a client works this way with an inner-child subpersonality. Temporary identification with a subpersonality brings immediate experiential awareness of that subpersonality's existence. This in turn can lead to the compassionate understanding of its needs, fostering the beginning of change towards its integration into the client's everyday life.

Mental imagery can also be used to bring about the symbolic resolution of conflict. Depending upon the content of the client's mental imagery, the counsellor will be sensitive to opportunities for the resolution of conflict. In the imagery she may intervene by suggesting to the client that she make some action, take a step forward or do and say something difficult. If this can happen on the level of the imagination, symbolically, the counsellor knows that it can also happen in the client's life. In mental imagery, for example, a client suffering from stress and nervous exhaustion discovered in her imaginative meadow an old, sick, tired, 'robot-like' character who begged to be cared for and to be allowed to rest. The counsellor encouraged the client to do this symbolically for the robot, which led to an emotional release with the client recognizing her obsessive tendencies. Of course, this realization then needed to be applied to the client's life situation and appropriate action taken to make changes

With mental imagery, two subpersonalities in conflict, like a critic and an achiever, can come to terms with each other on a symbolic level. With Anne, the counsellor guided her to imagine the two subpersonalities having a dialogue about their relationship, finding a way to get along better, and finally exploring the meadow together. Anne was able to experience that each had something to contribute to her life, but that each needed to allow the other to exist.

A third way in which mental imagery can be used for integrating subpersonalities is transformation. Mental imagery can be used to evoke and discover what is living at the core of a subpersonality, that which it ultimately has to contribute to the client's life, its transformed state. The counsellor may simply ask the client to visualize a subpersonality and enter into dialogue with it about its essential nature. In this way Anne discovered that her fourteen-year-old achiever would eventually have sensitivity and compassion to contribute to her life.

The counsellor may intervene with transpersonal images to help find the hidden potential of a subpersonality. Certain images like light, or symbols of ascent such as climbing a mountain, are traditionally used for evoking the potential transformation of a subpersonality and its subsequent healing. For example, guided day-dreams where the client climbs a symbolic mountain with a problematic subpersonality will often create a positive change during the climb. The client who discovered a child subpersonality chained up in the cottage brought the child out into the sunlight (a symbol for healing and regeneration) and took her up the mountain. By the time they reached the top of the mountain the child had developed into a young woman. When invited to have a dialogue with this young woman and allow her to reveal her essential nature, the client found her to be full of spontaneity and joy.

The counsellor may select the mental-imagery technique of seeking inner guidance by visiting a wise old person (a symbol for wisdom) in order to seek the contribution that a subpersonality can eventually make. With this technique the client is invited to imagine a wise old being who knows her very well, loves her very much and is available to guide her. She then can have a dialogue with this being, ask questions and receive answers about her subpersonality. This technique becomes more effective with continued use and, beyond immediate answers to problems, can become a source of self-support for the client.

Additionally, the counsellor can use mental imagery to create an ideal model of the client living her everyday life in a more harmonious way with a particular subpersonality. This, symbolically, builds an image which then tends to actualize itself. For example, a client suffering from performance anxiety imagined taking care of her fearful part by accepting and reassuring her. She then proceeded successfully with her performance rather than allowing her fear to immobilize her as she had done on previous occasions.

These more transformative interventions are most effective when complementing basic psychological work and are not meant as a substitute for it. If the client is in some way open to the transpersonal dimension, the above techniques nearly always open new vistas. If they do not, it is a clear indication to the counsellor that more work is necessary on a psychological level.

A second technique for subpersonality work, *gestalt identification and dialogue*, is, as described on p. 63, a potent and effective technique for the integration of subpersonalities. It is a principle of identification that, when the client identifies with a subpersonality, she reowns and includes that aspect in her psychological system. When two conflicting subpersonalities have a dialogue, their relationship can be improved. When using gestalt identification and dialogue, the counsellor will aim for this as well as intending that the client experience her identity beyond the conflict.

Third, the technique of *free drawing* gives physical expression to previously blocked psychological energy of a subpersonality. The counsellor provides crayons and paper and suggests to the client that she imagine how a subpersonality would express itself on paper. She is encouraged spontaneously to 'let it flow' without trying to draw anything in particular. This expression can enable the client to work more creatively with a subpersonality. For a more detailed description of this technique see p. 57.

Fourth and finally, the counsellor will use *disidentification from subpersonalities* as a primary technique for their integration. The extended development and use of this technique enables the client to: free herself from a particular subpersonality's domination and control; achieve a more objective view of it; understand its historical development; and find ways to heal its wounds. The principles and use of this technique are described in the next section.

SELF-IDENTIFICATION AND PSYCHOLOGICAL FREEDOM

Freedom of Choice

A strategy which covers all phases of psychosynthesis counselling is that of self-identification and psychological freedom which the counsellor holds as a long-term goal for the client. Working with chronic life patterns and subpersonalities fosters the client's recognition that her true identity is beyond the contents of her consciousness and her subpersonalities.

We all have an element within us that is permanent, consistent and unchanging although everything about us changes. Bodily experience changes, feelings come and go, thoughts flow by, but someone remains the same. Who experiences this incessant flow of the contents of consciousness? It is the self, or 'I', our true centre of identity. This point of self-awareness and volition acts as a unifying and integrating force within the personality.

The counsellor knows that a natural outcome of the process of the client learning to disidentify from subpersonalities or identifications is the emergence of the 'I' or personal self. What does this actually mean? It means that, little by little, the client can acquire an internal point of reference, a centre of identity which is beyond the contents of her consciousness; a place which is psychologically free, uncluttered and available at will.

As we saw with Caroline and Anne, without this centre the client will be *identified* with the contents of her consciousness. When Caroline felt impotent, she 'was' that impotency; if feeling angry, she *was* that anger; for Anne, when a moment of insecurity was present, she *was* that insecurity – and so on. Similarly, if we equate our identity with our roles ('I am a counsellor', 'I am a teacher', 'I am a mother', 'I am a businessman' and so on), when that role ceases to be, our sense of being is diminished. Whatever we are identified with consumes our consciousness, it dominates, controls and limits our awareness, perception and self-image.

Using the techniques described above the counsellor will seek to bring this state of being that is *identified* with a particular subpersonality or role into the client's awareness and help her discover how it limits her. Equally, the counsellor will aim to facilitate her to 'disidentify', to detach and to free herself in order to access more of her personality, resolve conflict and move towards her true identity. With the passage of time and with practice, this enables her to become more self-determining and autonomous. As one client said, 'I feel as if I have more space (psychologically) to move around inside myself and more power to choose what I know is right for me'. This statement reflects being disidentified from any particular state and having access to a wider range of experience and choice.

A natural disidentification occurs spontaneously through the client's work in counselling sessions. The counsellor's goal, however, is for this to become a deliberate and consciously willed practice. She will help the client to train herself to choose and to direct her identification at will. With awareness comes choice. With Caroline's discovery of her victim as a subpersonality came the possibility of change; she did not have to remain a victim. She could recognize it as a part of her, accept it and disidentify from it in order to free herself from its control.

Disidentifying from a particular element of our personality is not the same as 'distancing or cutting off'. All too many of us live unconsciously submerged in a particular subpersonality, role, thought or feeling. We are lost in a dream-like, semi-automatic state of consciousness. We are unaware. Liberating ourselves from an identification does not mean rejecting or abandoning it. To be consciously identified with an aspect of ourselves is quite another experience, and on the contrary, we become more alive and awake.

Fostering Identity and Psychological Freedom

Without a consistent sense of identity, there can be little self-acceptance or inner freedom. The client can eventually choose to identify with this centre in order to observe her experience and disidentify from limiting elements and behaviours. The counsellor's aim is for the client to learn this kind of masterful self-determination. How is this achieved and what techniques will the counsellor use to do so?

First, there is *observation*: in practice, as counsellor and client discuss and reflect upon her life, the counsellor is encouraging the client to begin to detach herself and observe. In order to talk *about* aspects of herself, she has to be one step removed. For example, through the counsellor's questions and interventions, Caroline began to *see* that she was operating from a victim consciousness. Another client discovered that her rebellious feminist was not all of her. The technique of gestalt chair dialogue also enabled these clients to disidentify and recognize their partiality.

A second technique which the psychosynthesis counsellor will use to foster observation and disidentification is *the Third Chair*. When the client is working with subpersonalities the counsellor may intervene with an additional empty chair. This chair represents a place in the client which is not the subpersonality or subpersonalities with which she is currently working. It symbolizes a detached observer who can compassionately and without judgement perceive clearly, and accept and offer suggestions. When Caroline observed her victim identity and saw how totally it had permeated her life, she was freer to explore alternative ways of being. With her victim now outside her she could begin to recognize that life could be more than suffering and tyranny. With the observer's advice she could also begin to find ways to heal the victim who had suffered much.

The counsellor used the technique of the third chair to enable Anne to recognize her ruthless critic who until then had remained totally unconscious. Anne thought that *she* did not like the adolescent. Finding the critic fostered the discovery that she had the potential to embrace the part of her left behind in childhood. Finding the critic also meant that Anne could be more tolerant and kind to herself in many areas of her life.

Third, using the technique of *disidentification* the counsellor will encourage the client to learn to disidentify and to take increasing responsibility for herself in action, words, thoughts and feelings. From this position she is able to see herself more objectively and with less distortions. The client *steps back* into the 'I', a stable place from which she can look at her life with a wider, more inclusive vision. Assagioli likened it to that which the Italians call belvedere, a place where our vision (and experience of ourself) is unobstructed; from which we can transcend the ever-changing contents of our personality.

The counsellor will, at the appropriate moment, use the educative function to teach the client these principles and introduce the technique of self-identification. As the counselling progresses into its middle phase, self-identification becomes relevant as the client outgrows old identities and behaviour patterns and is increasingly ready for the next developmental step. As we will see, however, transference may constitute a last regressive pull to inhibit her progress and maintain the *status quo*.

6

THE MIDDLE PHASE OF COUNSELLING

The initial phase of counselling often brings many insights and revelations which give the client a new sense of freedom. Furthermore, if the counsellor has become an adequate external unifying centre for the client, one which has mirrored her fundamental alrightness, the result will be an emerging sense of identity. Hopefully, the counsellor has modelled for the client the capacity for a broad perspective, an inclusive awareness and an empathic possibility for human relationships. This model eventually needs to be internalized by the client.

Our individuality, personal being or 'I', is profoundly influenced by an on-going empathic relationship with another human being. The counsellor provides this ground of being for the client as the client slowly finds her own. As we will see in Chapter 7, the client, more or less, develops an empathic relationship with her own Self. Our personal selfhood flows from this deeper source or Self, of which it is a reflection. The Self in psychosynthesis terms is framed as an organizing principle which provides directionality for our unfoldment and engagement with the world. As an *internal unifying centre* emerges for the client, a more conscious connection to one's Self, the 'I'–Self connection mentioned in Chapter 2, is strengthened.

Whereas in the first phase of counselling the sessions are a safe place in which to escape the chaos of life and finally be seen, heard and understood, in the middle phase, *the honeymoon is over*. The counsellor makes use of the 'testing' situations in the client's daily life to help her to implement her learning by making connections between her work in the counselling sessions and her everyday world. The counsellor aims for the process to deepen by shifting the level at which the client works.

For both counsellor and client, this can be a challenging and provocative period of the work. As the client learns that *the part* is not *the whole*, recognizes her identifications and reflects on her experience, she may begin to resist and reject this new-found freedom as too threatening and demanding. No matter how unpleasant, the known and familiar always feels safer.

Fear of a deep void or inner emptiness may accompany the potential loss of an identity. If this process is not rightly understood it can be overwhelming to face. Rather than perceiving this resistance as a set-back, the counsellor is alerted by it, knowing that it is a sign of the client's engagement. For example, if Caroline were not a victim, who would she be? Without his ex-addict identity, Paul felt uncomfortably vulnerable. Louise, the feminist, feared that to give up rebelling was to live in dead mediocrity. To each of them, a limited sense of self was better than no sense of self at all.

Although disidentification ultimately leads to inner freedom and a deepened sense of identity, clients may feel vulnerable without their old identity. Identities which we have had for a long time were initially developed for a purpose, usually as a way to cope with our life situation. They have served us well and provided some sense of meaning. To let go of them may feel like losing an old friend, a loyal soldier.

Assagioli (unpublished) warned of this potential resistance to disidentification as a natural part of the therapeutic process. He said that, 'to loosen the ties of identification which ordinarily bind the self to various elements of the personality and its relationship to others and the world, can create a sense of separation which is a normal and necessary step to becoming an individual'. This point was also made by Angyal (1965: 86):

Abandoning the familiar for the unknown always involves risks. When the changes are far reaching and precipitous they are bound to arouse anxiety. The anxiety felt at the prospect of dissolution of one's current mode of being has been related by some to the fear of final dissolution, of which human beings have the certain foreknowledge; since growth requires the breaking of old patterns, willingness to 'die' is a precondition of living.

SELF-IDENTIFICATION: THE 'I'

In the middle phase of counselling the counsellor's strategy is to continue the process of disidentification, but to shift the emphasis from the first phase of disidentification to the second of self-identification. This strategy places emphasis on the client again, internalizing the empathic mirroring the counsellor has provided and allowing the 'I'–Self connection to be enhanced. This actually leads to an increasing self-identification. The client comes to recognize that the source of strength, positive regard and self-respect is actually within her rather than in the external source of the counsellor. Psychosynthesis defines the self or 'I' as a centre of identity, of pure awareness and will. It is the place in each of us that is unchanging, constant and self-conscious. The 'I' provides a thread of continuity, although our experience of ourself and the world is always changing. It is the only part of us that remains the same throughout our life from beginning to end – the centre of our being.

The process of disidentification and self-identification is developmental and occurs throughout the therapy, regardless of what techniques are being used. It is the organic outcome of the client knowing herself more fully, and becoming more discerning about her behaviour. In time, as the skill of self-identification matures, we can learn to direct our identification at will.

Identification with predominant subpersonalities has already been discussed, but identification also occurs with psychophysical functions. For example some people seem to have an overall identification with their body and describe themselves in terms of physical sensation. Others are more identified with their feeling life. They talk about their state of being in affective terms, and live as if their feelings are primary. Yet others are identified with their minds and describe themselves in intellectual constructs. Psychosynthesis recognizes these functions as instruments of experience, perception and action – but not as our essential core.

Our consciousness is rarely free or naked, it is always coloured with a feeling, a thought, a role or a sensation which we tend to experience as our self. In the flow of the changing contents of consciousness, we lose our 'I'. Disidentification is the opposite; it is *remembering* that essentially we are a self. In addition, this self is the factor which differentiates us from others, provides us with a sense of 'I-ness' and evokes our individuality.

The Value of Self-identification

In psychosynthesis the 'I' or personal self is not seen merely as a place to reach, but an essential tool for psychological health. Ferrucci (1982: 67) writes, 'the self is not a reality to be experienced only with closed eyes. It is a realization that can be retained in the midst of daily life.'

A centre of awareness and will   Actively facilitating disidentification and encouraging the emergence of the 'I' is a valuable and practical strategy for the counsellor. As a means of developing the client's will, she will include opportunities for the client to make choices congruent with this goal. In the earlier example of Caroline, the counsellor evoked Caroline's 'I' in the following ways, which illustrate the methods that would typically be used. Caroline learned to make choices that enabled her to move beyond being a victim, and to assert herself. The counsellor achieved this by:

1   Encouraging Caroline to choose the focus of work for each session, and offering her a choice of techniques.
2   Shifting her identification away from the victim subpersonality by inviting her to spend *experiential time* identified with other aspects of herself. Mental imagery helped Caroline to envision and identify with the self-directed part of her. She chose activities outside the home, away from her children, which gave her freedom from being trapped.
3   Using their relationship, and moments when Caroline felt misperceived, moments of empathic failures, to repair the failure and further strengthen the client's emerging 'I'. This processing of empathic failures is an essential key to enable clients to work at deeper levels of themselves, as it gives them an abiding awareness that, no matter how difficult the human relationship becomes, it can be *worked through to a healthy outcome*.
4   Using ideal-model work for her to visualize her life as she would like it to be, and create a step-by-step programme to actualize this vision.
5   Reinforcing the behavioural changes she was making in her life; through active dialogue and helping her to see *how* (specifically what she said and did) she created these changes as a means of affirming her ability to do so.

Another illustration of how the counsellor facilitates disidentification is contained in the following example: the counsellor used mental imagery with a feminist client to take her to a meadow to explore other subpersonalities. Her intention was to help the client to find alternative parts of herself, thereby lessening her intense identification with being a feminist. Once the client had discovered the part of her that wanted to harmonize, and the one who appreciated beauty, she realized that she could choose co-operation as an alternative to rebellion. With another client who had a critic-adolescent polarity, the counsellor intervened with the third-chair technique, enabling her to find a place inside which was compassionate and to stop incessantly criticizing herself.

The will is a function of the 'I' and the activation of the client's will is an integral component in its emergence. The mobilization of the client's will is an extension of her commitment to heal herself, which enables her to integrate awareness gained in counselling into her daily life. In practice this evolution is the journey to individuality, and as such has successes and failures, peaks and troughs. The counsellor will, in subsequent sessions, follow up the attempted changes in the client's life. She will insist on working therapeutically with obstacles encountered to this actualization, so that what is or is not happening in the client's life becomes an essential part of the counselling.

Experiencing the 'I'   We usually experience our aliveness or sense of well-being in connection with a situation, circumstance, person or event. To experience the 'I' or essential self is to experience aliveness, independent of any structure, content or specific condition. The 'I' is not cognitive in terms of grasping a theory or understanding a principle; it is a direct knowing of a suprarational nature. It cannot be adequately described, it must be experienced. Carter (1978: 85) writes:

> to experience the 'I' requires a reorientation of our awareness towards its source; it is consciousness turning back on itself and becoming self aware. It is when consciousness is reflected back on its source – thus becoming true self-consciousness – that we finally realize our individual identity – It's me . . . I am this . . . I am aware – and become one with it.

In practice, this goal symbolizes a journey over a long period of self-identification work, and yet its value is immense. The 'I' is a difficult concept to grasp because it transcends the content of consciousness and, therefore, any words we might use would be inadequate. What follows are some descriptions from psychosynthesis clients, which help to point us in the right direction:

- From the 'I', I experience that I am totally free, unconditionally alive.
- The inside place that only I can experience; still, clear and always there.
- A space where I 'know' I am whole and wholeheartedly know what's right for me.
- I am just myself – deeply human, uniquely me, yet intimately connected to others.
- I am *at home* in myself with a deep sense of completeness and fundamental alrightness.
- When I am there, I am amazed that I haven't found it before – I tried to go out to seek it; yet it's always been there inside me.

A glimpse of such total being has left a mark on many clients. The discovery of the 'I', or even a fleeting moment of identification with it, can have several profound effects. In the realization that ultimately we *are* a self lies our true humanness, our unique individuality and our deepest sense of identity. In this state, inner conflict and fragmentation may temporarily cease, negative emotions which had previously plagued us lose their power, as we perceive them with a renewed sense of proportion.

As useful and inspiring as the experience of the 'I' is, the counsellor cannot create it for the client. It is the hard-won outcome of therapeutic work and practice. The realization may come in a momentary experience, but more often it emerges gradually. Beyond the ways mentioned above, there are several additional means by which the counsellor will support the emergence of the 'I'.

First, in *modelling the 'I'* by being an external unifying centre the counsellor demonstrates that it is possible to be non-judgementally aware, to have a perspective which is inclusive of the parts, to accept unconditionally and to provide a stable point of reference. The counsellor does this through her *presence*, attitude and behaviour with the client.

Second, there are *moments of stillness*: a value of the therapeutic environment is that it provides a place to be still, and learn to listen to our inner wisdom. The stress of modern life gives us little time to regenerate and we seldom create moments of quiet reflection, of *just being*. A psychosynthesis counsellor will intervene periodically by not just allowing a natural pause, but suggesting a quiet moment and emphasizing it.

At first this may be threatening to the client who may assume she has said something wrong. However, once understood, this pausing to become quiet in the session creates the ability to do so amidst the business of everyday life. Those who meditate will recognize this as similar to the stillness and inner focus generated thereby. This calm stillness can be a means of fostering a stronger sense of 'I'.

A third way of supporting the emergence of the 'I' is in *moments of being*. Whenever the client seems to have reached a more lucid awareness and is no longer distressed by a particular issue, the counsellor will invite her to spend 'experiential time' there. That is, she will ask the client to close her eyes and simply *be* where she is at that moment, without necessarily saying or doing anything. The counsellor will also invite the client to look again at her presenting issue from this more centred place in order to gain a better perspective. She will ask her to comment on what needs to happen, to give advice and to direct her own counselling work.

Fourth and finally, there is *active use of the self-identification exercise*. After a substantial amount of therapeutic work, the counsellor will use the educative function to introduce the existence of the 'I' and suggest consistent use of the 'self-identification exercise'. With clients who are willing to make the time and effort, this practice often yields striking results.

The counsellor's goal is not necessarily to have the client reach an experience of her 'I', but simply to move towards a more centred place. The client achieves an increasing sense of identity, glimpses the potential of one or becomes less overwhelmed by her difficulties. The use of this technique with an alcoholic client, who had never sought counselling before, helped her to discover a part of her which had choice about drinking.

With a client suffering from anxiety attacks, the counsellor suggested the use of the self-identification technique, first in the session, and then at home. While doing so, the client had an experience she described as 'erasing for a brief moment all self-doubt'. Later, when identified with her critic, the counsellor reminded her of that experience, which enabled her to free herself of the critic's domination. While working with a client who was obsessed with finding her life partner, the counsellor used the technique to help her discover that her well-being was not dependent on the relationship she so fervently sought.

It took Caroline a long time to have even a fleeting experience of 'I', but when she did she said, 'I never would have dreamt that *hopeless* me could find such a deep sense of value, of being an important part of this world and to know that I deserve to be loved.' The counsellor had achieved the aim of freeing her from the impact of her history. The self-identification technique evoked a right sense of proportion, enabled her to transcend the self-centredness of her victim identity and helped her to recognize that people were not against her.

By suggesting the self-identification technique with the feminist client, the counsellor intended her to experience the transcending of sexual identity. The client found herself in emotional turmoil when she realized that her true identity was neither masculine nor feminine. Following this insight, the counsellor asked her to imagine it symbolically. She visualized her feminist identity as an old worn coat hanging by the front door. Although it no longer fitted, she still put it on to go out. She felt naked without it. The counsellor then invited her to get an image for a place which was neither male nor female. This gave the client the impulse to let go of her limited perceptions of men and women. She said, 'Before being a female – or a male, for that matter – I am a self.'

Counsellor and client then discussed how she could reorientate her obsolete behaviour patterns. Her turmoil was alleviated when she discovered that her insight did not mean that she had to give up working for women's rights. She actually found that transcending mental constructs of gender made her more effective and enabled her to work with greater clarity. This is a clear example of the inner freedom which self-identification inevitably brings.

Assagioli (1965: 119) summarizes the meaning of self-identification in the fourth stage of his self-identification exercise:

> What am I then? What remains after discarding from my self-identity, the physical, emotional and mental contents of my personality, of my ego? It is the essence of myself – a centre of pure self-consciousness and self-realization. It is the permanent factor in the ever varying flow of my personal life. It is that which gives me the sense of being, of permanence, of inner security. I recognize and affirm myself as a centre of pure self-consciousness. I realize that this centre not only has a static self-awareness but also a dynamic power; it is capable of observing, mastering, directing and using all the psychological processes and the physical body. I am a centre of awareness and power.

In conclusion, it is important to stress again that the emergence of the 'I' or self-identity happens naturally and is a bonus of the therapeutic process. With the passage of time, the client recognizes that her problems and difficulties are not the whole story, and that there is a place within her which is beyond her pathology. In essence, the possibility of inner freedom is revealed to her as she increasingly learns to know and empathize with herself more deeply. The counsellor's guiding function diminishes as the client becomes more autonomous and capable of self-direction. The counsellor aims, over time, for this function to be gradually introjected by the client.

It would be unrealistic to expect, however, that self-identification would create instant integration of the personality or immediately promote psychological health. The principles that have been described in this section are an integral part of the counselling process and enhance its effectiveness as a resource to be used for the client's benefit.

THE HONEYMOON'S OVER

Even after the client has made significant progress and reached a degree of psychological freedom, she may become quite ambivalent about the work, her relationship with the counsellor and her own progress. Although it might seem incongruous with the awakening described earlier, resistance and transference are occurring. Freedom implies responsibility. Maslow (1967) described the avoidance of knowledge as the avoidance of responsibility, and asserted that knowledge demands action. This can evoke ambivalence in the client, who may react negatively and regress to childhood patterns of dependency. On one level insight and discovery prevail, while on another level the client appears to get worse. Her steps forward threaten the status quo.

The client needs to become aware of and fully experience her ambivalence and resistance before she can move through it. The counsellor should not gloss it over by reassuring her in an effort to alleviate her apparent disintegration. The counsellor will see this regressive reaction as an integral part of the client's process. She will remember that before the client sought professional help, she had probably spent many years developing sophisticated defence mechanisms to protect herself from pain. For example, the client may have avoided challenging situations, conformed rather than taken risks, somatized her anxiety and fear and deeply repressed her emotional responses. As the counselling becomes more effective, these defences begin to break down and this can be extremely threatening to her.

While this is an uncomfortable and challenging time for both counsellor and client, it is a crucial period in which the deepest growth may occur. The client is unknowingly confronting a basic fact of life – ambivalence – the tendency we all have to split and polarize the good and the bad, the positive and the negative in relationships, like the counsellor–client relationship. The client learns that life is not black or white, good or bad.

Through establishing and working through an empathic relationship with the counsellor, the client learns that her own self-worth and identity can include moments of difficulty and not be damaged or overwhelmed. Positive steps forward are seldom clear cut and rarely lie on the path of least resistance. Undreamed-of potentialities reveal themselves, previously insoluble dilemmas shift, inner conflicts are resolved but this may lead to resistance to the responsibility of further growth. If unprepared, the counsellor may find herself in a confusing mire of the client's ambivalence.

Transference

In psychoanalysis, transference neurosis is seen to be the centrepiece of the therapy. It is a state which exists between therapist and client which requires active confrontation, if the client is to be healed. Freud (1943) defined transference as the client unconsciously playing out childhood patterns by becoming emotionally and psychosexually fixated on the therapist. The client projects on to the therapist characteristics that she has in the past attributed to her parents, and relates to the therapist with similar attitudes, behaviour patterns and emotional responses. For further information on psychodynamic work with transference see Jacobs (1999).

Psychosynthesis views transference as a wide psychological field evoked in the client through her relationship with the counsellor. It is a composite of feelings, conscious or unconscious fantasies, remnants from childhood, unresolved conflicts, projections and behaviour patterns. Transference can be seen to be a 'new edition' of an old conflict, which means that it rarely is an exact repetition but a revised version.

Through transference, the counsellor may become the target of immense feelings of love, of rage, of seduction, of ambivalence, of dependency or of resentment. The client unconsciously attempts to *repeat* rather than to *remember* – believing that she really experiences these feelings towards the counsellor, rather than face the pain of remembering where they come from. This transference must then be interpreted and analysed for the client to experience formerly unconscious patterns in a conscious way.

The phenomenon of transference is not limited to the therapeutic relationship, but also occurs in everyday life. We unconsciously choose friends, mates, lovers and bosses who are likely to play assigned roles that as a child we attributed to important people in our universe. This underlines the immense value of working with transference in counselling.

Common forms of transference   There are several forms which transference universally takes and which appear again and again, although its actual content will vary from client to client. Some more common forms will now be discussed.

- *Love*: The client may feel love, admiration and sometimes sexual attraction for the counsellor. She may fervently desire to be the counsellor's favourite person, longing for a special relationship with her. Dependency characterizes this form of transference and the client may unconsciously resist growing up. It is wonderful to be loved and cared for by the counsellor. We see this in those clients who are very eager to please and try hard to be good clients. Beneath this seemingly positive transference is fear; the client unconsciously fears hostility, aggression or rejection from the counsellor.
- *Anger*: The client may harbour anger or resentment towards the counsellor, which is really her anger and resentment towards her parents, for what she either did or did not receive. She may be assertive, passive aggressive or rebellious towards the counsellor. She may come to sessions late, cancel at short notice, find fault with the counsellor, sabotage the counselling or even retrospectively devalue their work.
- *Fear*: The client, again unconsciously, may see the counsellor as an expert who has all the power and mastery that she herself does not have. With this type of authority transference, the client fears the counsellor, her potential rejection or being controlled and violated. The counsellor knows and has all the answers, is the model of health and potency, while she feels inadequate and incapable. This form of transference will be exaggerated if the client comes from a highly authoritarian family and/or has had negative experiences with dictatorial authorities in early education.
- *Idealization*: The client over-evaluates the counsellor as an ideal, superperfect person and places her on a pedestal. Rather than transferring negative and painful feelings on to the counsellor, the client is compensating. She creates, in the counsellor, a fantasy parent that she dreams of having. She imagines she has found this in the counsellor, who will love and approve of her and meet all her needs. The client seeks the security she lacks *outside* herself, and embodies an external source for the perfection for which she longs.

In addition, and inherent within transference, ambivalence is a common and tenacious aspect. In one counselling session the client will exhibit a seemingly positive transference, when the work is going well and progress being made, while into the next session she brings aggressive feelings and the impulse to stop therapy. This corresponds to Melanie Klein's idea that an infant will experience mother as two people, the omnipotent all-giving mother, and the inhibiting bad mother who frustrates her wants.

Transpersonal transference   The counsellor who works with clients on the transpersonal level has a double responsibility. On the one hand in the counselling relationship there is the lower unconscious, the past, where the client is likely to transfer in the traditional sense. On the other hand the psychosynthesis counsellor represents an explicitly transpersonal approach which involves superconscious energies. On this level, at times the counsellor may be a symbol to the client for the transpersonal Self, the timelessness, the beauty and truth that she has been longing for throughout her life.

The client may also project her positive qualities as well as her potential on to the counsellor. She perceives in the counsellor her own abundant goodness, capacity for intelligence and inherent gifts. With this 'projection of the sublime' (Haronian, 1972) there is substance which is authentic, but really belongs to the client. Naturally in the face of this extreme, the counsellor will eventually betray the client, as no human being could live up to it.

This betrayal rather than being a failure, carries an immense promise. It promises to lead the client towards the capacity to allow the therapeutic relationship to take a leap forward in maturity and wholeness. Through actively processing these difficult moments in their relationship, through being able to allow her counsellor to be human and imperfect the client learns to do likewise with herself. She is also, with her strengths and her weaknesses, nonetheless a worthy human being. The important point here is not that there should not be failures in the client–counsellor relationship, but that the sincere and open processing of these failures holds the key to the client's future well-being.

In the course of counselling there may only be traditional transference, or it may also be coloured and infused with transpersonal energy. If, for example, the transference is one of rejection, it is not only *mother* rejecting the client – it is also the *spirit* rejecting her. This is where the transference may be called archetypal, which is infinitely more intense, meaningful and painful than it would otherwise be. Here the counsellor must also be particularly aware of the pitfall of ego inflation and transpersonal aggrandizement, as the client may unconsciously expect her to be a spiritual teacher.

Strategy for working with transference   Although Assagioli (1967: 21) basically agreed with Freud's definition of transference and included it in psychosynthesis counselling, he stressed some essential differences in the importance placed on it and the strategy used to work with it. He considered it to be only one part of a larger, more diverse overall approach.

Reframing transference   Assagioli reframed the concept of transference positively, by viewing it as a healthy thrust of the organism to complete a gestalt, finish unfinished business and redeem childhood trauma. He saw the client's thrust as her unconscious and continuing search for unity. To elaborate this, we must go back to the starting place of our life, when we were in a total relationship with our mother. In the womb there was unity – no separation, total protection, fusion – all our needs were met. Of course this unity may be disturbed, and it is broken with birth which is the first separation we must survive. We all carry this early childhood experience of separation. There remains a part of us that still unconsciously longs for this unity and seeks to re-create it. The relationship with the counsellor carries an opportunity to redeem something lost – but now in a healthy way.

Counselling symbolically presents a similarly mothering situation. Angyal (1965: 179) described a therapist as a 'primal parent' to a defenceless client. In the consulting room the client is temporarily removed from her immediate worldly concerns. The counsellor is a person who gives total attention, presence and unconditional love. The world is once again seen as a potentially safe place. This can revive the distant longing for unity which re-energizes regressive childhood behaviour patterns. The client, seeking to reconnect, will tend to have the same responses and attitudes she had with parental figures.

This positive framing of transference enables the counsellor more readily to accept and include the difficult moments and to respond to the client more sensitively. It also fosters the counsellor's search for a more meaningful resolution of the transference by helping the client to find healthier, less dysfunctional ways of relating. How the counsellor does this is elaborated later in this chapter.

Consequently, the psychosynthesis counsellor views transference as an essential aspect of the middle phase of counselling. Her goal is to dissolve the transference as it emerges, rather than let it build into a full transference neurosis which is not encouraged, nor is it seen as the core of the therapeutic process. The counsellor's operating principle is directly to confront transference only when and if it becomes an obstacle to the counselling work.

Although initially there is often a positive transference, the counsellor may not address it, she will use the moment to build for the client an *external unifying centre* which models the client's future capacity for self-identification, to be in self-empathy, respect and positive regard. Unless it is extremely out of proportion, a positive transference can help to enhance the work in its early phases. The client will see the counsellor as competent and good, which aids the establishing of trust.

Jung (1954a) criticized Freud for saying that transference is universal, and saw it as only one of many therapeutic factors. Both Jung and Assagioli stressed the importance of the counsellor emerging from anonymity. Assagioli further stressed bringing the human relationship into the centre of counselling. He recommended that the heart of the work be based on I–Thou relating, in which self-responsibility is encouraged, and in which the counsellor is sincere and recognizes the strengths and qualities of the client. The psychosynthesis counsellor will relate to her clients in a less mysterious and detached manner than in classical psychoanalysis. These factors help to minimize the impact of transference.

As the personal relationship between client and counsellor becomes stronger, the transference will gradually lose its energy and will developmentally resolve itself, as the client goes through a process of maturation from child to adult. The counsellor needs to be aware of the transference, but it is often a matter of just letting it take its course. This idea is congruent with the view of Perls (1970), who said that the client will 'test' the counsellor by putting her in a parental position to see if she responds more adequately than her real parents did. If the counsellor passes the test, the client then moves through the stages from child to adult. However, in the adolescent phase, the client will need to become autonomous, assert herself in order to set boundaries and the counsellor must be prepared to 'live through' this developmental period with her.

Working with transference   Given the unique individuality of each client and the subtle, diverse shapes that transference takes, there is no unitary way for the psychosynthesis counsellor to address it. She will actively work with the client's unconscious elements which affect the unfoldment of transference by using a number of intrapsychic methods which require the wilful and experiential involvement of the client. The counsellor will continue to maintain the goal of strengthening the client's personal self, which promotes autonomy and inner freedom from regressive interpersonal limitations. This means the counsellor will work with transference both intrapsychically and interpersonally. She will choose from several methods to address the transference as it emerges, six of which will now be discussed.

First, as she learns about the client's childhood background and dynamics, the counsellor will anticipate potential transference. This *watchfulness* enables her to respond appropriately to the transference as it emerges. She will consistently ask herself, 'What kind of mothering does this client need, and expect? Am I in any way colluding with the client's negative parental patterns?'

A client whose childhood was so deficient that she lacked the potential for self-support will need to go through a period of dependency on the counsellor. Through being an external unifying centre the counsellor serves as a positive emphatic model, in order to provide the client with an exemplary pattern. The counsellor is willing to 'carry the transference', but will aim for the client to become self-sufficient as she develops a more stable identity.

Second, to enable the transference to be abated, the counsellor will encourage the client to work on her parental relationships. The counsellor will aim to resolve the client's intrapsychic conflict using techniques like gestalt identification and dialogue. For example, the counsellor will invite her to imagine her mother imagos (the mother which she carries inside) on an empty chair and begin to have a dialogue with her. Through the therapeutic process of identification, the client becomes aware of the dynamics with her mother and gradually releases her parental introject. Coming to terms with her relationship to her parents can prevent the same dynamics being transferred on to the counsellor.

To complement this work on negative parental relationships, the counsellor often introduces a reparenting technique to the client. Using mental imagery she helps her to develop a nurturing inner parent. For example, a client who had been abandoned by her mother filled the void by building an image of an ideal mother, whom she visualized and with whom she identified for a period of time. This practice reinforces but cannot replace the confronting of the pathology.

As well as addressing parental relationships, a third way to address the transference involves the counsellor engaging the client in subpersonality work with her inner child. After all, it is the inner child who actually transfers onto the counsellor. For example, with a client who had been abused as a child, and was suffering from depression and self-destructive behaviours, the counsellor sought to uncover through mental imagery the 'wounded child' whose growth had been stunted by the traumatic experience. She encouraged catharsis with the imaginative reliving of early experiences of abuse. Through listening and dialogue, she helped the client to establish a subjective relationship with her inner child, and to respond to her needs.

Another way to achieve this, is for the counsellor to ask the client to bring to a counselling session photographs of herself as a young child. The counsellor would encourage her to dialogue with the child in order to evoke maternal feelings towards herself, which can then be elaborated, expressed and built on.

The counsellor's long-term goal is for the client to care for the wounded inner child and to provide, from her own inner resources, the parenting which every child deserves and rarely has. Replacing negative parenting with the client's provision of good parenting lessens transference neurosis and builds her capacity for self-nurturance.

A fourth method for approaching the transference involves the counsellor following two guidelines when addressing transference. To begin with, she will aim to evoke the transference pattern into the client's consciousness. She will achieve this by exploring with the client her feelings towards her and the dynamics of their relationship. She will help the client relate her feelings to similar ones she has felt at earlier times in her life. The counsellor will pursue questions like: Are these feelings familiar? Have you felt this way before? What is the history of these reactions?

The counsellor then aims to prevent the transference from repeating itself by providing the means for the client to change her interpersonal behaviour. For therapeutic reasons, the client often needs to re-experience her limited responses from childhood and to release repressed energy. It is also important that the counsellor does not unknowingly collude with the transference by responding in ways similar to those of the client's parents. Through their relationship, the counsellor will encourage the client to explore behaviours that were unavailable to her as a child, and to establish new and healthier modes.

Some case examples will help to illustrate this point. A client, who had been abandoned by her parents, experienced rage when the counsellor went abroad to tend to a gravely ill family member. Although aware that her feelings were irrational, she felt the counsellor had also abandoned her. Her pattern for dealing with this in childhood had been to withdraw and deny her needs. On this occasion she did it again. The counsellor noticed her withdrawal and invited her to explore how she *really* felt about her absence. She encouraged her to do what she could not do as a child – express her rage. This enabled the client to experience that she could express her anger without risk of further rejection, which helped to dissolve her reaction.

Another client's transference took the form of idealization, until she had a dream in which the counsellor was not paying attention to her and had cut a session short. The counsellor knew that the client had convinced herself how wonderful her mother was and had created numerous justifications for her mother's lack of presence. Using mental imagery, the counsellor guided her to re-experience the anger she really felt towards her mother for not being there when she needed her. For the first time the client was able to accept her resentment without feeling guilty, and to begin to perceive the counsellor as human.

Another client's transference was one of love and dependency. She strove to be a good client, to please and placate the counsellor, and withheld anything for which she imagined the counsellor might judge her. She was deeply afraid of rejection, and unconsciously refused to grow up and take responsibility for her life (as this would mean separating from both mother and the counsellor). The counsellor drew her attention to her 'pleasing behaviour' and encouraged her to begin to risk authenticity. As the client discovered that the counsellor would not reject her for being human, she could accept herself in a similar way.

Fifth, transference may also reveal itself through a seemingly unrelated image that the client has. Desoille (1965) suggested that the client's attitude towards the counsellor may emerge in a less threatening symbolic way. One client dreamt of a Nazi soldier pushing her into a crevasse. The counsellor asked who the soldier reminded her of, and she promptly replied, 'You'.

Although this client had appeared to be very co-operative, her Nazi image told it all, and enabled them to explore how this behaviour was a repetition of her relationship with her father. The counsellor's goal was to empower her ability to choose whether to co-operate or not. She achieved this by frequently inviting the client to notice the motivation and the quality of her co-operation.

Alternatively the counsellor can use mental imagery to work through the transference symbolically. Rather than ask who the Nazi reminded her of, the counsellor could use imagery to explore and resolve her relationship with her. Coming to terms with the Nazi would reveal how she could also come to terms with the transference. The symbolic resolution would then be interpreted and applied to the client–counsellor relationship.

A sixth and final way of addressing the transference involves the psychosynthesis counsellor recommending to the client the periodic assessment of their work. These reviews provide the opportunity for a deeper exploration of their interpersonal dynamics and the counsellor will be watchful for hints of transference. She might challenge behaviours she has observed in the client, confront unspoken feelings and evoke unexpressed communications and hidden resentments.

Countertransference   Assagioli (1967: 71) stressed that the counsellor must not lump all client responses into the transference construct, but must use discrimination to examine and assess their validity. A component to the client's transference may actually be an empathic failure, where for a moment the counsellor lost her centredness and did not perceive the client wholly. Empathic failures are inevitable in any relationship, for none of us are perfect, including the counsellor. It is not a therapeutic tragedy if an empathic failure occurs. It is a tragedy if the counsellor avoids sincerely addressing the failure and views it as merely a transference issue. For it is in the successful processing of empathic failures that the client learns about authentic intimate relating.

It is also true that the deep wounding of the client that has emerged can trigger the counsellor's own deep wounding. This has been called a traumatic countertransference (Firman and Gila, 1997) and requires the counsellor to have worked on her own psychospiritual journey and addressed her own pain and suffering. Otherwise the counsellor will be unable to discriminate between what is her own material and what is the client's.

The counsellor must look within herself for her own affective response to the client, in effect, her countertransference. For instance, if the client feels judged, the counsellor must search for these feelings towards the client. In the safety of the counselling situation, the client may also be 'trying out' new behaviours that she is learning. For example, if she has previously conformed in order to win approval, the first place where she may begin to be assertive is in her relationship with the counsellor (as a prelude to doing so in life). This behaviour could be misinterpreted as transference.

Transference should not be addressed without also recognizing countertransference and the impact it has on the counselling relationship. In psychosynthesis, countertransference is the wide psychological field that is evoked in the counsellor in response to the client. It includes the counsellor's emotional reactions, unconscious fantasies, expectations, anxieties, hopes, unresolved conflicts and remnants from her own biographical history. For example, if the client professes love for the counsellor, how is she to react? She may feel invaded, upset or embarrassed. Conversely, the client may be meeting the counsellor's own unfulfilled needs for love and intimacy, or her need to be an authority, and thus she may encourage the client's dependency. Perhaps she will cheat and take it personally: 'Of course it's transference, but I'm also a great counsellor.' Some people unconsciously become counsellors in order to redeem their own traumatic childhood, or to heal their own wounds or to become the parent they never had. The counsellor needs to be alert to her degree of involvement and identification with the client.

Some but not all of the countertransference may belong to an earlier part of the counsellor's life. As with transference, countertransference is not always pathological, but can be an authentic human response to the client. The counsellor must examine her relationship with the client for 'blind spots' and historically repetitive behaviour patterns. The transpersonal context of psychosynthesis trains the counsellor to maintain her ability to perceive the client as an inviolable Being with immense potential. If she loses this perception, she will need to confront that in herself which stops her from fully accepting the client as she is. It is a gift to see the beauty that is always there in a client in spite of all the difficult moments.

Counsellor feedback of her own internal responses to the client can also be valuable in the counselling arena. For example, if the client is working through a pattern of significant people in her life rejecting her, and the counsellor perceives her unconsciously sabotaging their relationship, she can use this response creatively by challenging her.

The counsellor may also experience emotional responses to situations from the client's past which are really the client's repressed material. She may experience a feeling like grief or anger which belongs to the client, who has repressed it. To communicate this response can enhance empathy and open the client's eyes to those feelings in herself. If the counsellor feels inadequate to serve the client, these feelings may be her own inadequacy or may be a reflection of the client's feelings of helplessness.

The counsellor's response to the client can enhance and further the course of the counselling. At other times, a more neurotic countertransference may be operating which will inhibit the counselling relationship. Here the counsellor will find herself caught in emotions, attitudes and impulses towards the client which resemble those experienced with significant people from her own past. These represent her blind spots and as such can impede the work. If the counsellor feels either a strong negative or positive response to the client, such as hostility, boredom, love, anxiety or impatience, she needs to examine her countertransference reaction.

If the counsellor finds herself feeling stuck with a client, she may well discover that her countertransference is the problem. When she confronts her countertransference, the freedom will arise for her to deal with the transference more skilfully. Transference need not be a problem unless there is an unconscious countertransference. In supervision, for example, a counsellor explored feelings of impatience towards a young male client who was dependent upon her and whom she felt was not moving quickly enough. A countertransference insight revealed that he reminded her of her younger brother who had, in her opinion, never actualized his potential.

Countertransference can take a wide variety of forms, of which the following are some examples:

- giving longer sessions than is useful to the client;
- never challenging the client for fear of losing her love;
- avoiding confrontation out of her own fear of anger;
- believing the client's positive transference to be true;
- unconsciously using the client's dependency to feel powerful;
- fulfilling her needs for intimacy;
- giving unnecessary advice out of a need to be an authority;
- overvaluing the client's progress for her own success.

It is essential for the counsellor to know well her own psychospiritual organism in order to discriminate her responses. She must be able to discern what content of the counselling relationship is an authentic response to the client and what is her own biographical material. The counsellor needs to have therapeutic resources available for dealing with destructive countertransference, through supervision and her own psychotherapy.

It is too easy, in a book of this nature, for the counselling relationship to appear to be a clear and systematic issue. In reality transference and countertransference quickly become complex and pervasive, being difficult to identify and unravel, and even experienced counsellors easily make mistakes. Jung (1954b) described the counselling relationship as a state of mystical participation – a mysterious underworld phenomenon – which in reality is filled with uncertainty and creative chaos. With this Assagioli wholeheartedly agreed.

SUMMARY

We have seen that the middle phase of counselling includes both the emergence of a deeper sense of identity and a resistance to that emergence, both natural elements of the client's increasing wholeness. It is both a creative and challenging phase for the counsellor which requires that she deepens her own commitment to the client's well-being. It is a period where the client's external life should begin to reflect her counselling insights as she implements them into behavioural change. Transference may or may not be a focus of this phase, but it requires the counsellor's conscious awareness.

If the counselling thus far has gone well, both counsellor and client can be satisfied as they move into the final phase of their work together. However, in this book we have not yet addressed the very heart of psychosynthesis counselling – the transpersonal dimension. The transpersonal realm will be operating implicitly throughout the counselling and from time to time be explicitly visible. The next chapter will focus directly on this very essential aspect of psychosynthesis counselling.

7

THE TRANSPERSONAL DIMENSION
OF COUNSELLING

People are hungry for truth, goodness and beauty, but today they often do not know where to find them. Both in our culture and in psychology it is difficult to talk about the transpersonal dimension. Our spiritual lives have become as embarrassing to us as sexual lives were to the Victorians. Until recently our scientific bias has limited us to quantitative and statistical exploration. In spite of numerous accounts of the experience of a higher reality found in all ages, cultures and disciplines, we are reluctant to admit the existence of the non-rational and of spiritual values. The inadequacies inherent in our language and the difficulty of communicating the true nature of transpersonal experience have added to this. Finally, we are afraid to acknowledge a world so very different from the everyday one, particularly one which is at times baffling and riddled with distortion.

In spite of the above realities, Transpersonal Psychology is beginning to make its mark on the therapeutic mainstream. In the 1990s the British Psychological Society formed a new sub-section of transpersonal psychology; psychosynthesis professional training centres acquired university validation and now issue degrees in psychosynthesis; the European Association for Psychotherapy recognizes the field and there has been an increase in public interest. Consequently people seeking a better quality of life see counselling as a means of addressing their deeper needs – for meaning and purpose, for fulfilling an inner longing, a *divine homesickness* for a better quality of life.

Interestingly enough our culture today is witnessing a number of distortions in the transpersonal field of human experience. An awakening may occur within individuals whose personality is not integrated enough rightly to benefit from it; and to over-identify with it can lead to a renunciation of the value of the everyday world. Confusion of levels can cause ego inflation which sometimes results in fanatical behaviour and the formation of cults. The association of spirituality with religious dogma has driven many away from the transpersonal dimension. However, these distortions themselves symbolize a *reaching out* for something beyond the personal. Yet it is understandable that many approach the field of transpersonal psychology with caution and trepidation.

Freud saw the desire for something beyond the personal as neurotic – a regressive tendency to return to the undifferentiated primal unit of our mother's womb. Assagioli criticized Freud for labelling man's higher values and achievements as adaptations of lower instincts and drives. Assagioli maintained that these higher impulses, desires and motives exist in their own right, develop whether or not the aggressive and sexual drives are satisfied and have their own source, a centre of spiritual identity.

Assagioli (1973) reminded us that in Western psychology, souls are out of fashion and have been so for a considerable period of time. He stressed, however, that the transpersonal domain is not a religious one, and claimed that the reality of spiritual experience and higher values is independent of the formulations of religious institutions. Assagioli with psychosynthesis, Jung (1954b) with analytical psychology and Frankl (1973) with Logotherapy spent much of their lives researching and exploring the ways in which desire for something greater than ourselves is intrinsic to human experience. They believed that acknowledging the spiritual dimension is crucial to seeing the individual as a whole person and that transpersonal experience influences inner reality and outer behaviour.

TRANSPERSONAL PSYCHOLOGY

Transpersonal psychology is a response to and a modern initiation of the search for wholeness beyond the bounds of a person's individuality, and leads to an exploration of consciousness, creativity and inspiration, values and meaning. Ferrucci (1990) shows that support for the principles of transpersonal psychology has been coming from researchers and scholars in a wide spectrum of disciplines: comparative religion, the psychology of creativity, physics, philosophy, social analysis, systems theory, anthropology, neuropsychology, mythology, altered states of consciousness and near-death studies.

It is not the purpose of this book systematically to explore the field of transpersonal psychology but to illustrate its principles and practice in counselling. The characteristics of transpersonal psychology that are relevant to this purpose are:

- It postulates in man the existence of a spiritual centre of identity, the Self, which includes the personal dimension but goes beyond it, and that both the experience and expression of this Self fosters evolution.
- It recognizes that human relationships are of central importance and that *relationship* is the means for realizing oneself through valuing the fundamental identity of the other. The journey to this capacity is through an individual's own primary 'I'–Self connection. (See Chapter 6.)
- It systematically explores the realm of human potential by addressing experiences of superconscious content, either those descending into the field of consciousness or those found in the process of ascending to transcendent levels – creativity, intuitive insight, superconscious revelation, mythical and archetypal realms, and altruistic imperatives.
- It accepts that spiritual drives or urges are as real, fundamental and indispensable as the basic psychological ones, and that these higher needs for self-realization must be met for optimum health. Within this context its goal is to enable the client to meet physical, emotional, mental and spiritual needs appropriately in accordance with individual temperament. Hence, no one principle, method or technique is correct for everyone.
- It suggests that each person benefits from identifying a purpose in life which is meaningful and potentially fulfilling.
- It reframes crisis, pain and pathology as opportunities and challenges for growth and creative steps forward and holds that they are intimately connected with a person's self-realization.

THE SELF AND THE SUPERCONSCIOUS

Assagioli (1976) likens the three principal stages of psychosynthesis counselling to Dante's *Divine Comedy*: first, there is the descent into the Inferno, which represents the psychodynamic phase of descent into the lower unconscious; then the journey through Purgatory which resembles working with the client's existential reality; and finally the ascent to

Paradise which symbolizes exploring the transpersonal dimension of the psyche. As we have seen, establishing a stable centre of identity and of inner mastery is an aim of personal psychosynthesis and the focus of the initial and middle phases of counselling. A balanced emphasis on the development of self-identity provides the psychological stability for an exploration of the transpersonal domain. And this journey is never simple nor linear, but rich with interdependent cycles, changes and movement.

The 'I' is intimately related to the Self. More precisely, it is a projection or reflection of the Self, an outpost of it in the personality. The 'I' is that small part of the Self with which our waking consciousness is able to identify at any moment. It is the *'I–Self'* connection that gives us our unique sense of *personhood*, linking our spirituality with its human aspects. A wounding or break in this connection will cause a rupture in our deepest sense of who we really are – a true 'soul wound' (Firman and Gila, 1997). It is the healing of this 'I'–Self connection and the restoration of which that is essential to transpersonal work. It is also essential to recognize this because to attempt to reach the transpersonal dimension by bypassing work with personal identity is an error. The emergence of the 'I' is precious and often the result of a long period of evolution and should not be discarded. With good intentions, but at the cost of great conflict, many try to destroy the personal 'I' for transpersonal pursuits.

The goal in psychosynthesis counselling is not to reach the transpersonal dimension as a *place to get to*. Transpersonal work is a *process* to be experienced which can greatly assist both counselling and psychological health provided we understand its nature and purpose and place it in its correct relation to the whole. Figure 1 illustrates Assagioli's (1965: 17) model of the human psyche and helps to clarify the distinction between the personal self and the transpersonal Self (identified simply as the Self throughout this book).

1   *The lower unconscious* corresponds to what Freudian psychology calls the unconscious: the fundamental drives and complexes charged with intense emotion and so forth. This realm has been discussed at length in Chapter 1.

2   *The middle unconscious* is formed of psychological elements similar to our waking consciousness, containing the memories, thoughts and feelings of which our everyday life is interwoven. This awareness is accessible to us by tuning in or remembering, and contains recent or near present experiences. It points not to what we have been or could be, but to the evolutionary state we have actually reached.

1 The lower unconscious
2 The middle unconscious
3 The higher unconscious or
   superconscious
4 The field of consciousness
5 The conscious self or 'I'
6 The higher self
7 The collective unconscious

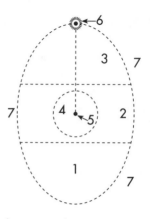

FIGURE 1 *Assagioli's model of the human psyche*

3 *The higher unconscious*, or superconscious, is the 'home' of our higher aspirations and intuitions, latent psychic functions and spiritual energies. This includes artistic, philosophical, scientific or ethical revelations and urges to humanitarian action. Assagioli attributes to this realm the source of the higher feelings (such as compassion, joy), of genius and of states of contemplation. illumination and ecstasy. Most of us have had, at some time, a moment of superconscious experience when we felt most fully who we essentially are.

4 *The field of consciousness* contains those elements of our personality of which we are directly aware. This includes the incessant flow of sensations, images, thoughts, feelings, desires and impulses, which we may immediately and consciously observe, analyse and judge.

5 *The personal self* or 'I' is the centre of our consciousness, a point of pure self-awareness and will. As we have seen, this centre is distinct from the changing contents of our consciousness.

6 *The transpersonal Self* is the point of pure, essential being which is unaffected by conscious experience. It is not an experience but the *One* who experiences, the *Experiencer*. The personal self is considered to be a reflection of the Self and its projection in the field of the personality. The Self is the point of synthesis of our whole being, of individuality and universality, or our connection with the larger whole of human existence.

7 *The collective unconscious* can be defined as the accumulated psychic environment that surrounds us. The boundary that separates us from it is permeable. It is analogous to the membrane delineating a cell

which permits a constant and active interchange with the whole body to which the cell belongs. Such processes of 'psychological osmosis' are occurring all the time between human beings and their environment.

Differentiating the Self from the Superconscious

The Self is an 'ontological reality' which exists on its own level as a stable centre of life and the source of superconscious energies. The Self is like the sun which does not move relative to the earth. It is the centre of our solar system, pervading it with its radiance and sustaining and holding it together through its attractive force. In this sense the Self is a *field* of energy containing phenomena of a superconscious nature, and providing the conditions for evolution development and growth. Maslow (1971: 266–7) writes:

> this is a special phenomenological state in which the person somehow
> perceives the whole cosmos or at least the unity and integration of it
> and everything in it, including his Self. He then feels as if he belongs by
> right to the cosmos. He becomes one of the family rather than an
> orphan. He comes inside rather than being outside looking in. He feels
> simultaneously small because of the vastness of the universe, but also
> an important being because he is there in it by absolute right. He is a
> part of the universe rather than a stranger to it or an intruder in it.

Although the Self is unchanging in its essence, it sends out its energies which are stepped down in intensity, transmitted through superconscious experience, and received, absorbed and utilized by the personality. How effectively the personality expresses these energies is dependent upon the degree of personal integration, hence the value and importance of psychological work. The difference in these three aspects of a person is one of level rather than nature.

The Self is pure Being. It is contentless and transcends superconscious experience and expanded states of awareness. All superconscious experience has content; there is always movement, feelings, actions, visions, ideas and so on: it is a qualitative experience. Although these states are more difficult to define than everyday experience, we can still do so. Superconscious experience often precedes awareness of the Self and consists fundamentally of becoming aware of the activity which occurs on higher levels of the psyche. Joy and love for all living creatures, the creative flashes of the artist, the fulfilment of helping others, sensitivity to beauty and intuitive insight are all examples of superconscious experience.

To have a true experience of the Self, however, it is necessary to disidentify also from the superconscious. This is very difficult because superconscious states can be so joyous and meaningful that we easily become attached to and identified with them. Maslow called this diversion 'higher sidetracking'. The field of transpersonal psychology often fails to make this important distinction. Peak experiences are deeply fulfilling and often illuminative, and, if properly understood and integrated, are of significant value in the counselling process.

THE VALUE OF THE TRANSPERSONAL IN COUNSELLING

The revival of interest in the transpersonal today is triggered, on the one hand, by an increasing dissatisfaction with competitive materialism, the pursuit of immediate gratification and, on the other hand, by a conscious or unconscious search for different and higher values and activities, a longing for what is largely termed spiritual. In earlier times we more easily accepted ourselves the way we were, and identified with family, class, locality or nation. But today, with far greater mobility and communication and the breakdown of some social institutions and national boundaries, these secure identifications fall away and we are thrown back on to ourselves. This experience leads to existential anxiety and a search for more than a transient stability. We are hungry for beauty and goodness to enter our lives; especially hungry are those who seek counselling and suffer from the soul wound.

In working with the transpersonal in counselling, it is not productive to think in terms of strategies, but rather in terms of hypotheses, principles and techniques. Just as the counsellor cannot *create* a sense of identity for the client, no strategy will necessarily lead to an inner awakening or personal transformation. There is much that can be done, however, to remove the obstacles to such experience and to create the psychological climate for its emergence. Most importantly, the counsellor, through their *relationship* can mirror the client's fundamental alrightness, enabling the client to internalize their own connection to Self, inevitably evoking an awakening to the transpersonal. If there were a strategy, it would only be to create the space and provide the opportunity for the client to include the transpersonal dimension of her being.

Transpersonal work in counselling is not a substitute for psychological work but rather a vivifying and practical complement. The timing of it is important because the counsellor cannot begin to work explicitly with the transpersonal, or systematically explore potential, if the client is in deep crisis or submerged in her suffering. It is here that the counsellor *must* foster an empathic relationship which models for the client her own 'I'–Self relationship as the first condition necessary for any regeneration. However, when the client is able to observe herself and reflect on life experience, the counsellor can intervene by directing her attention to other modes of her being. Alberti (1975: 4) tells us:

> guided by the therapist the patient thus acquires knowledge of the existence of other modes apart from his symptoms, and experiences them existentially. The experience reveals to him that, in the first place, he is not his symptoms but has symptoms; and, secondly, that symptoms are not his only experience; he has many other experiences as well . . . he meets with an expansion of consciousness, not in a downward direction in search of the origins of his disturbance, but rather upwards, to find aims and values that, in making life worth living, attest to the validity of a cure.

A Transpersonal Context

A counsellor working in a transpersonal context recognizes the pivotal role of consciousness in determining the outcome of counselling. Consciousness is both the instrument and the object of change, and the counsellor will be less concerned with *problem-solving* than with fostering the conditions in which the problem can be addressed creatively. Rather than resolve a particular situation in the client's life, the counsellor supports her while she learns *how* to deal effectively with her problems as they arise.

Working from a transpersonal context also means that, regardless of technique, through the therapeutic relationship of empathic holding and mirroring, the counsellor has taken a *stand* for basic human goodness, placed her trust in the client's fundamental alrightness and is willing to accompany her on her journey to wholeness. This context fosters a transpersonal element in the counsellor and client's relationship – so essential for sincere and successful counselling. The ground on which they stand together is rich with the necessary components for the client both to heal herself and move progressively forward.

Transpersonal experiences arise at any time, often spontaneously and when least expected. There are various modalities through which the contents of the superconscious emerge into consciousness – through intuitive insight into one's problems, through the imagination and images which carry a positive charge, through inspiration and its subsequent creative expression or through illumination which reveals the essential nature of life and its true unity. The counsellor who holds a transpersonal context will use these moments to further the client's work on herself by responding to them and encouraging their elaboration.

Addressing Problems on Two Dimensions

A psychosynthesis counsellor will aim to address and explore the client's difficulties from both a personal and transpersonal perspective. Essentially, there are two ways to work on her presenting issue: psychologically, in the ways described throughout this book, and by using transpersonal principles and techniques.

Rather than having the attitude of getting rid of the client's pain, the counsellor asks herself: Why? What is the purpose here? What potential is contained within this problem? Where can this lead us? This 'why' is not a psychoanalytic why into past causes, but one which reveals future possibilities. This attitude fosters transcendence enabling the client to perceive her difficulties from a different, more inclusive perspective. It also fosters the client's ability to embrace the immanent, the inherent learning available to her.

At an appropriate moment, the counsellor will introduce the transpersonal dimension, both to assist the process of personal integration and to go beyond symptom resolution towards transformation. The following case examples illustrate this.

A client, whose twin sibling had died at birth, sought counselling because throughout her life she had experienced deep self-hatred and shame. Through psychological work she discovered that she was angry about her twin's death and finally came to terms with her mother's rejection of her. To include the transpersonal dimension the counsellor initiated mental imagery for the client to reconnect with her dead twin in order to explore what remained deeply unfinished in this situation. During this she spontaneously relived 'womb experiences' of joy and unity. The counsellor furthered the imagery work by intervening with the transpersonal technique of seeking inner guidance through an image of the wise old being. The being advised her that she was not responsible for her twin's death, that she had unconsciously believed that she too should have died and that she had projected her positive qualities on to her twin. It was only when the counsellor included the transpersonal realm that the client had these deep realizations which resolved this life-long problem for her.

A client suffering from a rare and incurable disease sought counselling to come to terms with both her illness and a traumatic childhood which included sexual abuse. After working psychodynamically on her relationship with her mother for several months, the counsellor wished to assess their progress. Using mental imagery she asked the client to find a symbolic image for that relationship. She saw a map of a battle with red and blue flags denoting the warring factions. The counsellor initiated the transpersonal technique of shining a beneficent light on the image to reveal a potential resolution.

Some dramatic changes took place. A river flowed through the centre of the map, dividing it. On the client's side was a peaceful landscape. On her mother's side a battle still raged. Suddenly the client cried, 'I can't let this separation happen; if I do I'll be as cruel as my mother. Something's missing! My heart is missing!' At this point she experienced severe pains in her chest and started sobbing. The counsellor again intervened with a transpersonal technique by inviting her to see within the light her own Self which was available to assist her. Spontaneously an inner voice spoke to her of the need to love herself first and foremost, and to separate from her mother. At this point the client underwent a vivid physical change. Her breathing became relaxed, the pain in her chest ceased and her skin took on a warm glow. She felt that at last she had come alive. Following this experience the client's health improved, she felt more detached from her mother and mourned her lost childhood.

This rather lengthy case example demonstrates how transpersonal work can be both transformative and physically healing. It also reveals the resources of the human spirit in its ability to heal itself in seemingly impossible circumstances. Transpersonal work can be inspiring to both the counsellor and client.

Working with Transpersonal Qualities

Clients will often present their problems on a practical level rather than a qualitative or subjective one. For example, 'Should I quit my job?' 'Should I leave my partner?' Rather than searching for the *right* answer, a psychosynthesis counsellor will focus the client on the qualities that underlie these questions. There is a subjective level behind every issue which can enable the counsellor to work beyond the mere resolution of symptoms and problem solving. The counsellor will explore with the client what quality is emerging through her difficulty.

Once the immanent quality is established much work can be done to recognize and accept the quality, work on the obstacles to its emergence and nurture its development and expression in the client's life. For example, if leaving her job would give the client more freedom, the counsellor would acknowledge her need for freedom and explore what stops her from being free. The client may be fixated on leaving her job, when the real issue is her need for freedom. Besides leaving her job, there are many other possibilities for creating more freedom, such as learning to assert herself, or developing the capacity to enjoy herself more. In the end, she may or may not choose to leave her job.

The Systematic Exploration of Potential

A fifty-year-old man came to psychosynthesis counselling after years of psychoanalysis. Although his life had improved tremendously, he was still plagued by a deep sense of insecurity and self-doubt. Aware of his therapeutic history, the counsellor used several transpersonal techniques (described below) to foster his sense of life purpose and self-expression. This led to the client choosing a different career path, one which he felt to be closer to his heart. Six months later he was a transformed person. His needy clinging to others for affirmation was gone. His insecurity was reduced considerably and he began to trust himself more with the effect of, as he described it, 'standing more solidly in myself, in my own integrity'.

Vaughan-Clark (1977) writes that from a transpersonal perspective, each client, as well as being in conflict and stress, is seen as having the capacity for self-healing and for manifesting qualities and capacities which are latent or undeveloped. In psychosynthesis counselling, at an appropriate moment, it is valuable for the counsellor to encourage the client to explore her sense of potential and her ability to express herself creatively. The purpose of doing this is to integrate the client's work on her problems with a more positive thrust, enabling her to realize that she has all the needed resources within.

Transpersonal techniques often stimulate the client's own capacity to heal herself and are used to complement basic psychological work. They are not, however, an alternative to more straightforward counselling work and would be ineffective if used to avoid confrontation with pathology and pain. It is advisable for the counsellor to work towards the client's personal integration before initiating a systematic exploration of potential.

Exploring Life Purpose

No amount of purely psychological work will be sufficient to provide the client with a deeper, more meaningful sense of life purpose. To know that there is a significant direction, a tacit unfoldment and the potential for a fulfilling life can encourage and hearten the client while strengthening her motivation.

A sense of life purpose will tend to naturally emerge as the client increasingly affirms the connection between personal identity and their deeper Being. As the *soul wound* is healed, as the client experiences a sense of connectedness with the Self within, life begins to take on a new meaning. In eastern philosophy this is called *dharma* – that within the individual and for each of us there is an ideal life pattern or purpose. It can be likened to a seed. Just as the seed of a flower contains the blueprint for the flower which the seed will become, and inherently knows *how to become* that flower, there is a similar *knowing* to be found in the depths of our humanity. You don't have to *teach* a seed how to become a flower just as, given the right inner conditions, the immanent knowing of life purpose is accessible to the client.

Taking the analogy one step further, if a seed of an oak tree tries to become a rose bush, it has a problem. It won't work. We all know the experience of trying to be something we are not – because someone told us to be that way or because of childhood conditioning which we have internalized. It is only through the restoration of our connection to our deeper Being that our own unique seed (I-amness) can blossom.

Once the client begins to envision themselves in a new way, the counsellor can support this process through the use of transpersonal techniques. Various guided day-dreams may be used to provide the client with a sense of purpose. There are many such structured experiences for this type of symbolic exploration. The day-dreams themselves merely provide a subjective experience of the higher thrust of the client's life and further require the active use of grounding and expressive techniques (see p. 62). Here are a few examples of these guided day-dreams.

The hero (or heroine's) journey to find a hidden treasure is symbolic of the client's path of unfoldment. We find a similar metaphor in Ulysses' Odyssey. In the experience of taking this journey, much about the client's spiritual path is revealed and valuable insight is gained from the process of the journey itself. The treasure, if found, symbolizes what is most essential to the client at that moment in her life and its meaning is considered important.

In many cultures the flower has been regarded and used as a symbol for the spiritual Self. The blossoming of the rose exercise is figuratively associated with human experiences of evolution, which imply passage from the potential to the actual. It is surprisingly effective for stimulating transpersonal awareness in the client as she dynamically visualizes the rose's transition and development from closed bud to fully opened bloom (Assagioli, 1965: 213).

Another exercise, adapted from the work of Ira Progoff (1975), is 'the road of life'. The client begins by spending time reflecting on her life and the many crossroads she has experienced, the way she has crossed them and the values underlying the choices she has made. With mental imagery she is then invited to travel symbolically the road of her current life but instructed to meet a crossroad leading into the future. She explores travelling in each direction and is subsequently helped by the counsellor to interpret their meaning and its relevance now.

The guided visualization of a sphere with many concentric circles, each representing a layer of the client's being, provides information regarding the layers of her personality. To reach the centre of the sphere is likened to reaching the centre of the Self. The counsellor suggests to the client that her goal is to travel through the different spheres without getting stuck at any one sphere, and to reach the core of her being, her spiritual Self. Her experience is then appropriately interpreted and its meaning illuminated.

One client found the following layers: one of her life with her family; another of her professional role as a teacher of dance; a third as a member of her larger community; a fourth of herself searching and learning from life's experiences; yet another layer of her personal odyssey and deep relationships, warm and pulsating with a feeling of longing; next came an image of a tiny naked being, full of potential energy and pushing into an erect stance; and finally, a small golden heart with a vast space in its centre – enclosed, yet connected to an infinite space. Of this experience she said, 'I felt that this was the ultimate core of my being. I experienced an enormous sense of peace – mentally, physically and emotionally. '

More practically, the counsellor can ask the client to imagine, in the best of all possible worlds, how she would like her life to be five years ahead. What would be important to her? What qualities would she like to be expressing? What values would be her highest? Mental imagery would be used symbolically to explore the answers to these questions and visualize them in detail. Together counsellor and client actively translate the figurative responses into concrete meaning and action in the client's life.

Free drawing may be used in conjunction with mental imagery work to explore life purpose. The client is first asked to get a symbolic image in answer to a question and then to draw her subjective experience of the image. A series of questions like the following are used:

- Who am I?
- Where do I come from?
- Where am I going?
- What's in my way?
- What do I need to develop and nurture in myself to get there?

As usual, time will be spent with client and counsellor interpreting the meaning of the images and drawing and applying it to the client's everyday life.

TECHNIQUES USED IN TRANSPERSONAL WORK

The counsellor often uses the technique of mental imagery for transpersonal work. Mental imagery is an indirect or symbolic process, an intermediary step, which requires detailed interpretation and grounding. Imagery works well because it is abstract, as is the nature of inherent potential. Conversely, understanding potential requires intuitive insight as opposed to rational explanation. In combination with imagery work, the counsellor uses gestalt identification for the purpose of intrapsychic integration which helps the client to elaborate and integrate the potential she is uncovering (see pp. 54, 57 and 63). The technique of free drawing may be added as a complement and provides a form of expression at any time during the work. To culminate transpersonal work, it is essential for the counsellor to help the client to implement behavioural changes which are congruent with her discoveries. The primary value of transpersonal work is gained through its being actively grounded in the client's everyday life. The ultimate goal is for the client's life to become an embodiment of her deepest experience of herself. (See 'Grounding and creative expression', Chapter 3, p. 62.)

There are several additional techniques which the counsellor offers to explore the client's emerging potential and impulse for creative self-expression, four of which will now be discussed.

The Technique of Inner Dialogue (Assagioli, 1965: 204)

Each one of us has within a source of self-love, understanding and wisdom which is in tune with our unfolding purpose and clearly senses the next steps towards its fulfilment. The counsellor will aim for the client's development of the capacity to find her own answers, to be self-sufficient and to trust her inner wisdom. For example, with cases of sexual abuse, the technique of evoking a wise woman with whom the client can enter into dialogue is effective at uncovering what is needed in order for healing to take place. The wise woman can provide her with an ongoing source of inner guidance regarding how to move beyond these experiences.

The counsellor often uses the inner-dialogue technique to address the client's existential difficulties. The idea that a source of integrity is available within the client is congruent with Buber's (1971) teachings on inner dialogue and I-Thou relating. Through the counsellor's relational modelling of an empathic connection between personal identity and Being (the 'I'–Self connection), the client will eventually internalize this experience. The counsellor's goal is for the client to relate intrapersonally in a similar way.

This technique is simple and straightforward. The counsellor invites the client to close her eyes, relax and breathe deeply, and imagine seeing the face of a wise old being (a man or woman) whose eyes express great love for her. This being knows her very well and is in touch with her deepest elements. If this is too abrupt, the client can be introduced to the technique with imagery work of imaginatively climbing a mountain and finding the wise being on the top. The top of the mountain is symbolic of ascending to the heights of our being.

The counsellor then encourages the client to engage this wise being in a dialogue to help her understand her difficulty more clearly, and to ask relevant questions regarding directions or choices she is facing. However, the communication between the client and wise being may also happen symbolically without words.

Alternatively, the counsellor may invite the client to choose her own symbol for wisdom. Common images associated with this source are: the sun, a diamond, a fountain, a star or point of light, or even sometimes a particular animal.

With this technique the client is making contact with universal archetypes which are in the higher collective unconscious, by means of their reflection or projection into her own superconscious. Assagioli defined these archetypes as universal principles which unify, heal and give meaning. The wise being is traditionally used as an archetypal symbol for wisdom.

The answers which the client receives are the result of transcending the rational mind and liberating creative aspects which are usually blocked. It is similar to the creative process of wrestling with a problem, going as far as possible with it and then simply waiting for a solution to emerge.

Given the nature of the human psyche, however, the counsellor will not encourage the client blindly to follow insights gained through using the technique. Any inner message can come from a variety of sources as well as the superconscious, including the lower unconscious, unfulfilled needs and desires combined with various degrees of distortion. The counsellor values helping the client learn to discriminate between those images which carry true wisdom and those which do not. For example, occasionally a critical and authoritarian figure will appear which is a projection of a sub-personality or her super-ego. It is also possible for the client to project on to the superconscious the message she *wants* to hear; or depending upon the transferiential relationship, provide answers which the client imagines the counsellor would wish to hear.

The counsellor will focus the client on the correct interpretation of insights and information gained through the inner-dialogue technique. The message received is not always clear and time will be spent on its clarification and application. The concrete application of a particularly abstract or symbolic answer will need to be extracted and utilized. Conversely, the client may receive a simple but profound answer which still needs interpretation. This will be achieved through reflection and dialogue, followed by grounding and creative expression.

When using inner dialogue the answers may not present themselves immediately. Asking questions is as important as seeking answers, because the client's intuitive processes are stimulated and the insight may come at a later time, often unexpectedly. It may also come in unusual forms, such as an impulse for action, a sudden intuition, the right words from a friend, in a book or a song. In time, the need for a symbol may become less necessary and the wisdom will come through an inner voice, which is trustworthy and available to the client to inform and guide her.

Evoking and Developing Desired Qualities

The counsellor will aim for the client to cultivate and nurture chosen transpersonal qualities. Certain qualities are needed when confronting an obstacle or resolving an issue and this technique provides a transpersonal method for doing so. The counsellor elicits the choice of quality from the client. It can be used, for example, to evoke courage in fearful situations, love in interpersonal relationships or strength in times of crisis. Working with transpersonal qualities is based on the principle of evoking archetypes and their regenerative ability.

The counsellor will guide the client to develop a mental image of herself possessing and expressing this quality. Time is spent creating a detailed image of herself with which she is invited to identify. The counsellor then takes it a step further by asking the client to visualize herself displaying this quality in a real-life situation where it is especially needed.

Following imagery work, the client will experiment with expressing the quality in chosen areas of her life. As she attempts to do so, the counsellor follows up how this process is working, its results, successes and failures. Together they actively address her experience to enhance its actualization. Hence the development of a desired quality evolves from the subjective visualization to its objective manifestation.

In a minority of cases, the client may experience an adverse reaction to this technique. This indicates that there is a core of negative emotion that blocks development of the desired quality. Rather than framing this as a failure, it leads the counselling to precisely the area requiring attention.

The Ideal Model

This technique has been described in detail in Chapter 3, and its application is both personal and transpersonal. The transpersonal component always envisions potential and that which is possible for the client. It is most valuable for helping her to conceive what she wants from the counselling work, and her goal for the resolution of her difficulties. It is also used to enable the client to create a realistic and attainable self-image, in order to replace a poor or distorted one. The ideal model is not an ultimate model of perfection but rather represents the client's foreseen direction.

Meditation

For practical purposes, meditation can contribute to mental development, a clearer sense of identity and transpersonal exploration. Its use evokes a relaxed, purposeful and focused atmosphere which encourages the deepening of perceptivity so useful for transpersonal work. It can enable the client to go beyond set patterns and mental habits by giving birth to new ideas and insights.

Meditation, as used in psychosynthesis counselling, can be defined as a form of *inner action*. Far from being an escape from life, meditation can provide a means of looking at it in a new and deeper way. By re-uniting the client's inner and outer world it helps inner experience, outer perception and behaviour become more congruent.

Like all forms of practice, meditation requires discipline; one has to learn to use the mind in a conscious deliberate way. It is also a matter of finding the appropriate mental tone: if we are mentally forceful or harsh, our mind becomes rigid and crystallized. However, if we let our attention wander, we lose the capacity for clear and insightful thinking.

Meditation can be used in counselling in two primary ways. First, *reflective meditation* requires directing the activity of the mind on to a chosen topic, to think deeply on it and examine its various levels of meaning, not just giving a superficial glance at one or two of its aspects. The process of engaging the objective faculties of the mind allows it to become subjective, to probe in a deeper way than usual and to evoke intuitive understanding. By *deep thinking* on a subject the client gains a clear, experiential idea about it, and through persistent and sustained attention comes to know it *from the inside*.

Here the counsellor suggests that the client meditate on a transpersonal quality she would like to awaken or strengthen in herself, like courage, love, openness, joy and so on. It is also an effective way of reinforcing a positive quality that is emerging. This form of meditation follows the principle that energy follows thought, and meditating on these qualities will tend to evoke them. At times it may also energize the obstacles to that quality in the client. This is a natural occurrence which provides the opportunity to work further and resolve them. The ability to use the technique of reflective meditation also provides the client with a resource for work on herself outside the counselling arena.

The client is first instructed to relax and breathe deeply. The counsellor then invites her to take a few minutes to reflect, out loud, on all that she is aware of about this quality. (If done at home, the client writes her reflections throughout the meditation.) This stage is called reflection or pondering. To ponder on the quality involves focusing one's thoughts carefully in order to penetrate its deeper meaning. The counsellor may ask the client questions like: What does this quality really mean to you? What are all the different aspects of it? Where in the world do you perceive this quality? What would you and your life be like if you possessed more of it?

Following the period of reflection, the counsellor will suggest to the client that she spend a few more minutes being silently receptive for further insights and awareness to reveal themselves. They may come through words, images or symbols. Together they will discuss and clarify the resulting awareness in the client and how it can be applied to her life situation.

The second principal way of using meditation in counselling involves *meditating on symbols* evoked through mental-imagery work. Such meditation can deepen and elaborate as well as greatly enhance the effect of that image on the unconscious, and may assist in resolving inner conflicts and in transforming negative tendencies into positive ones.

In a way that is similar to reflective meditation, the counsellor invites the client to hold a chosen positive symbol steady in her mind and reflect on its meaning. The client may also be asked to identify with the symbol, to speak as the symbol of its essence and nature; and if appropriate, to establish a two-way dialogue between herself and the symbol. For example, in a counselling session a client spontaneously had an image of an oak tree, solid, strong and stable (as she wished herself to become). The counsellor guided her to meditate on this oak tree both in the session and later at home in order to strengthen its potential emergence.

The Creative Use of Pain and Crisis

For many people, the most growthful times of their lives are moments of pain and crisis. It is in these moments that we are potentially most open to learn and in these moments we tend to seek counselling. In times of crisis our personality is less firmly organized, old structures are collapsing and we are more vulnerable – all of which contribute to the opportunity for working creatively with pain and crisis.

Personal trauma can deeply damage a person and lead to states of psychological rigidity and depression, but it can also lead to insight and regeneration. Which of these alternatives occurs depends, not on outer circumstances, but on the inner response of the individual. Assagioli (1975: 12) stressed that sooner or later we are obliged 'to face up to reality and try to understand the meaning and value of the obscure and apparently negative aspects of life'. He recommended a dignified but not dispirited humility in the face of the mystery. We need only look around us to see that life contains a continual disruption – chaos, birth and death, beginnings and endings, integration and disintegration – to see the wisdom of Assagioli's attitude.

A transpersonal view of acceptance   Often we cannot change outer circumstances but we can always change our inner response to them. This will depend upon the attitude we bring to our situation, the value we ascribe to it and whether we choose to utilize it. Creatively embracing pain and crisis requires a heartful acceptance in order to collaborate with the inevitable, 'bless the obstacle' and transform it into a stepping-stone.

The kind of acceptance we need for this is beyond our everyday responses of passive resignation or tolerance . It warrants a dynamic act of will to apprehend the deeper meaning in the crisis and to grasp our essential spiritual liberty. Rebellion and striving to eliminate pain and crisis merely tightens the hold it has on us. It is better to bestow it with meaning, include it as an essential part of our purpose and embrace its potential to serve us.

Transpersonal acceptance is based on the principle that higher consciousness is not dependent upon any external situation or circumstance. As soon as we stop running away from pain and can look it in the face, transformation can begin. Crisis can be seen as an integral part of the larger whole of our lives and can contribute to our growth towards the next level of consciousness. It is the 'keeper of the gate' to new awareness.

A woman sought counselling for psychosomatic symptoms of heart palpitations and a stomach ulcer. After several months of counselling the counsellor suggested mental-imagery work to explore psychological correspondence to the ulcer. She guided the client to imagine becoming very small and to travel into her stomach. There the client discovered an old crone whose grief had been suppressed at the time of her husband's death ten years previously. This old woman evoked the client's compassion and she was able to accept her grief. With this discovery the ulcer began to improve.

The counsellor then facilitated a process of 'grief work' using transpersonal techniques to explore what had been important to her in her marriage and what qualities (gifts) she wanted to take from her relationship with her late husband and bring forward into her present life. The counsellor helped her develop these qualities and form an ideal model of their free expression. Working to express this ideal model she began within a few months to express the joy, harmony and vitality her husband had symbolized for her. As a side-effect of this work the client's physical symptoms dissipated.

Paradoxically, an often neglected side of transpersonal acceptance is one of embracing the unknown and respecting the mystery of life. Our minds incessantly, and often desperately, seek to rationalize and under-

141

stand our experience when at times this is not possible. The counsellor may encourage the client to accept the uncertainty and abandon the attempt to wrap her crisis up into a neat and tidy package. The client often needs reassuring that it is OK just to let it happen and that value comes from experience itself. The counsellor's ability to convey this is dependent upon her own attitude to uncertainty and pain, and upon her ability to trust the process.

Transcendence of pain and crisis   Transcendence can be a healing and regenerative function which cuts through the psychological mire, at times bypassing the need for painstaking step-by-step work. It can shift the context in which we experience our disturbance, rather than working endlessly with its content. Whereas our normal life is full of contrast, conflict and dichotomies, in a transcendent experience these divisions crumble and reality becomes a unified whole. Duality can melt as the transpersonal allows us to see beyond good and bad, past and future, ourselves and others, rational and/or emotional and to perceive with a consciousness which can include both.

Any transpersonal technique can lead to an experience of transcendence and often does, although this is not their primary goal. Self-identification work encourages transcendence and nurtures it as a skill for life. The counsellor holds transcendence as both a long-term goal and an intended result of transpersonal work and uses the self-identification exercises as a direct method for achieving it. In this sense disidentification, for freedom from psychological limitation, and self-identification, for transcendence, are both a personal and a transpersonal method. As the client strengthens her 'I'–Self connection, she acquires the skill of being fully in the moment *and* perceiving fully, as well, a wider perspective. This in turn provides a *freedom of choice*, for the client.

The immanence of pain and crisis   Working transpersonally is not necessarily about 'going somewhere' but concerns the consciousness with which we perceive what is in the existential moment. It is a process to be lived, not a goal to be achieved. The transpersonal is also immanent, inherent within pain and crisis, and involves an expansion of consciousness which embraces and co-operates with the emerging potential. The redemption of pain and crisis requires the counsellor to help the client perceive and receive its gift.

Psychological disturbance is often a response to the transformation process. That which limits us and causes us to suffer can become the source of our greatest strength. It can be of great benefit to question the deeper meaning of a crisis to discover how it is ultimately serving us. On occasion, the counsellor asks the client questions like: If life were teaching you something what would it be? How can you use this crisis to serve you? What step forward is contained within it?

These questions enable the counsellor to reframe the client's experience. For example, with a social worker who had worked for years on her traumatic childhood, the counsellor pointed out that her parents had given her a thorough preparation for her work in the caring profession, the best training possible in fact. Through her negative experiences with them she had to develop compassion, sensitivity and trust in the possibility of change. The counsellor's reframing 'hit the mark' and, for the first time, the client let go of the pain of her deprived childhood. Another client, who was trying to stop smoking, had managed to cut down considerably but was unable to give up. The counsellor reframed this crisis for her by commenting on how great it was that she had gone from forty cigarettes a day to five, which focused her on success rather than failure.

Gordon-Brown and Somers (1988) stress the importance of perceiving the client's symptom as a symbol and exploring its meaning. If, for example, the client experiences a psychosomatic problem, what is its message? If plagued with consistent feelings of inferiority, is the client really inferior, or perhaps the symptom is providing her with the opportunity to transform her self-image?

PROGRESSIVE AND REGRESSIVE PAIN AND CRISIS

We sometimes put ourselves in situations or circumstances which we know will cause a crisis but which honour our next step or respect our sense of potential. The pain of choosing such a step, however, is a progressive one. Some examples of progressive pain are: a career change in the midst of success; terminating an unhealthy relationship after many years; changing to be more honest and assertive. The crisis generated by such choices is one with meaning and value, and by its progressive nature will be easier to resolve. It is alive with a deeper movement and contains the thrust of the transpersonal.

On the other hand, a regressive crisis carries the pain of resistance – of saying 'no' to growth and change and making life choices which betray our potential. Our limitations control us and we are their victim. Something new is trying to be born through an unwilling channel.

Examples of regressive crisis are: staying in a career that is unfulfilling because of fear of change; allowing neurotic needs for security to justify remaining in an unhealthy relationship; avoiding the threat of rejection by conforming.

Regressive pain reflects being prisoner to our past and prevents us from moving forward. It holds no benefits. We only lose when we sell out on ourselves. If not dealt with creatively and transformed into a progressive crisis, regressive crises repeat themselves again and again. Something is knocking at our door and if we do not open it, it knocks each time with greater vehemence. For example, a client seeking counselling for relationship difficulties will often be repeating the same behavioural patterns. An addictive personality will manifest addiction to many things. Some people are consistently unable to risk departing from the norm, although their values would lead them to do so.

The existential crisis   Without the developmental step of expanding individual identity beyond personal existence, Frankl's (1970) 'existential crisis' or crisis of meaning tends to emerge. Although relatively integrated and appearing to live a more or less successful life with many goals achieved, a person's life can begin to lose its lustre and become grey and meaningless. The things that were once rewarding are no longer so.

This crisis challenges the very meaning of one's existence and for some can be extremely painful and disorientating. This is not neurosis, for often the individual has attained a level of functioning readily called 'normal' by modern mental-health standards. But once an individual can stand on her own two feet, what does she do then? Just stand there? She may ask herself 'big' questions like: What am I here for? Is this all there is to life; there must be more to it than this? What is my place in the world? These pertinent questions may arise at any stage of counselling.

Without undue emphasis on finding the right answer, a psychosynthesis counsellor will take these questions seriously and help the client to explore them. The resolution of the existential crisis occurs when the client is able to expand the meaning of her existence beyond the boundaries of her personality. The existential crisis is an opportune time to seek or to renew contact with the transpersonal dimension, and indeed can be seen as a progressive impulse to include it. The counsellor helps the client to do so by directing her attention towards her transpersonal nature and by offering any of the transpersonal techniques thus far discussed.

The inclusion of the transpersonal dimension can take many forms. For some clients, superconscious energies may spontaneously erupt, sometimes with great intensity resulting in an inner awakening which becomes a major, life-changing experience. More often, the reorientation is gradual and requires the client's conscious and purposeful participation. Often with this awakening comes a *remembering* of past transpersonal experiences which, due to a lack of validation at the time, were suppressed and undervalued. Their return to consciousness provides a natural opening to the transpersonal dimension so essential for relieving existential crises. Again it must be stressed that the counsellor will not seek to reach any particular goal but to help the client uncover what is meaningful and relevant to her. There is no right answer.

The crisis of duality   While some individuals experience the existential crisis with more or less intensity, others have its seeming opposite, the crisis of duality. With the crisis of duality (Assagioli, 1965: 46–9) the client has a broad vision of inherent meaning, of how life 'could' be and of the immense potential of human existence. The problem is often that she has insufficient psychological integration to cope with this vision, and consequently feels frustrated by her inability fully to express it in her life. Too much awareness of potential can lead to excessive perfectionism and a desire to force oneself and one's life to conform to it. It can also lead to a sense of guilt and failure for not measuring up to one's own expectations. The result may be a tyranny of the positive and a resistance to existential reality.

The crisis of duality is a progressive crisis and as such is fundamentally an opportunity for growth. Its resolution is by continued work on the personality for the purpose of developing the capacity to actualize vision and meaning. A sense of right proportion (and patience) must be established between the individual's experience of a transpersonal vision, the scope of its expression and its implementation in the world. The counsellor first encourages the client to explore subjectively and define this and then to set about the task of actualizing it in a realistic and effective way. Both personal and transpersonal techniques will be used to confront obstacles as they arise.

A similar form the crisis of duality can take, but different from a lack in one's capacity to express the transpersonal, could be termed *visionary tyranny*. Some individuals have an unusual capacity to consistently experience and perceive the existential moment from a very wide and global perspective. Awareness of many levels of meaning can lead to an individual being *driven* to transform each moment into its highest possibility. Once that potential is achieved, yet even greater levels will reveal themselves, leading to a lack of fulfilment. This can happen particularly for those who have achieved a high degree of psychospiritual integration. A client who ran a successful charity sought counselling because she could not allow herself to rest. There was too much need in the world, too much suffering and her awareness of this meant that she could never allow herself to stop – always driven to do more. For this client, the cultivation of the qualities she called 'visionary common sense' brought great relief.

LONGING AND RESISTANCE: THE REPRESSION OF THE SUBLIME

Endemic in our culture is both a longing for the transpersonal, a conscious or unconscious search for the sublime and a pervasive resistance to it. The counsellor knows that in working with the transpersonal dimension, the client is seldom free of ambivalence. Both Jung (1933) and Assagioli (1965: 47) recognized that we suppress and deny our higher nature and our potential while at the same time yearning for them.

Maslow (1968) wrote of existential guilt; the more we are conscious of these positive impulses, the more shame we experience at our failure to express them. This is not a neurotic super-ego guilt, but guilt for not being and living as we could. Haronian (1972: 10) emphasized that psychoanalytic thinking provides an easy escape from this guilt, 'which can reduce the call of the higher unconscious to nothing but the sublimation of the impulses of the lower unconscious'.

Fear of the Sublime

We fear the challenge of transpersonal growth because it means abandoning the familiar for the unknown, which always involves risk. The anxiety which arises at the potential dissolution of our present way of being unconsciously reflects the final dissolution of death. Something in us may need to die, however, in order for us truly to live. The willingness 'to die' psychologically is as unfamiliar to us as is physical death; we go to unbelievable lengths to avoid facing it. We are being called upon to abandon our cherished illusions. Although common in Eastern teaching, the mystery of surrendering oneself in order to find oneself goes against modern rationality.

There are many poignantly human reasons why we avoid fully realizing our higher nature and deepest aspirations. To embrace the transpersonal can stimulate many fears and resistances. It evokes fear of the personal responsibility involved, and the burden of an awakened conscience. If our psychological integration is a hard-won achievement, we fear losing this precious individuality.

Identifying with our essential Self and our superconscious strengths implies becoming powerful in the true sense. Such potency can evoke a fear of power, especially if we have ourselves been prey to its misuse. It is safer and more secure to remain weak and impotent.

Fear of change and disruption can accompany consideration of one's life purpose. We may, from within, be called upon to live differently, with contrasting values to our previous ones. Inertia seduces us to maintain the status quo – change is hard work. Beneath this inertia often lies a fear of being alone. If we fully answer the call of the transpersonal, we fear becoming different from everyone else and therefore alienated.

Those who have worked through a super-ego complex often fear the domination and authority of the Self. This authority may feel unfamiliar and be perceived as a controlling outside force. Our freedom is threatened and we risk replacing the conventional super-ego with a spiritual one – full of higher-order 'shoulds', the tyranny of the sublime – not realizing that this inner authority will liberate us.

Feelings of inadequacy and fear of failure can be stimulated by the experience of our immense potential. A basic insecurity towards the Self causes us to doubt our own worthiness, not realizing that here lies our true source of self-love and validation. We unconsciously feel that we do not deserve such beauty and light.

Finally, for many, a fear of letting go and trusting (surrender) is evoked by transpersonal experience. There was a time in early childhood when we *ran to life with open arms*, and for most of us this trust was betrayed. The promise of the transpersonal reminds us of this deep trauma and can evoke terror.

Defence Mechanisms Towards the Transpersonal Dimension

There are many defence mechanisms which enable us to escape the threat of our fears of the transpersonal dimension. Repression of the sublime is the most common, in which we are not even aware that the transpersonal exists. We unconsciously force our higher nature into the darkest recesses of our psyche and pretend it is not there. We deny our essential being and identify with our personality

Projection of the sublime provides us with a convenient way to 'export' our positive qualities on to others, often the counsellor. We see our higher Self, our own beauty, creativity, intelligence and giftedness in others, thereby eliminating the effort of managing it ourselves. If we see in another person our own higher nature, we do not have to be responsible for it and can continue in the comfort of being the person we have always been.

Transpersonal experience can elicit the contrary reaction, of what seems to be its opposite, compensation. The counsellor sees this defence mechanism where, in one session, the client takes a significant step forward or has a transpersonal experience, and in the subsequent session becomes very aggressive and distressed. This response, although unconscious, is a desperate cry of the personality to remain the same.

Rationalization, a common defence, empowers us to explain away transpersonal experiences. We find plausible reasons why these experiences were merely a momentary illusion or a hallucination. We can be very skilful at finding a variety of reasons not to accept the transpersonal.

Regression distorts the transpersonal realm and creates an easy means of avoiding responsibility. In this case we accept the sublime but perceive it in a regressive way by unconsciously imagining that the superconscious will provide the solution to all our problems. We delude ourselves that the transpersonal brings a ceasing of all effort and conflict and that all our needs will be taken care of.

Negation, the most simple of all defence mechanisms, readily closes the door on transpersonal experience. We simply deny that it exists. We disaffirm the sublime, make it unreal and our disregard prohibits its emergence.

Finally, retrospective devaluation allows us to diminish the transpersonal experiences that we have had. We may have a very beautiful superconscious occurrence and later make it insignificant and unimportant.

Confronting these resistances as they arise is essential in psychosynthesis counselling. The counsellor respects them as the client's need to maintain psychological stability while remaining sensitive to their effects. As with any defence mechanism, they slowly reveal themselves, and the client's self-discovery is the aim. Once the client is conscious of a defence mechanism, the counsellor will intend for her to experience how it limits her, to become aware of its cost and to choose to let it go. Any technique of psychosynthesis may be used to transcend and move beyond these defence mechanisms. Eliminating the repression of the sublime occurs step by step, as the client increasingly integrates her personality.

148

Service

Although we have seen the value, as well as the promises and the pitfalls of the transpersonal realm, no discussion of this vital arena of human experience is complete without presenting the concept of *service*. Over many years of practising psychosynthesis, I have seen again and again that, as an individual increasingly touches their own deeper Self there arises the impulse to also touch others. The client may recognize that she is not an isolated unit, but rather a relational being in constant interaction with many diverse relationships. Competition becomes co-operation. Conflict becomes arbitration and agreement based on an understanding of what Assagioli (1973) termed *right relationship* – interpersonally, socially and globally.

A strengthened '*I*'–*Self* connection leads to the capacity for love, empathy and compassion. Clients consistently have reported that they feel both the need and the desire to give something back to life and to contribute to the well-being of others. This is not 'do-gooding' or a social conscience, but rather a centred, mature reflection of good will. Once awakened, an individual begins to make life choices which are consistent with the welfare of others and the common good of humanity. One may feel *called* to take actions which are an expression of good will.

There is no particular form or forms which service requires – it can be expressed through any activity of life – and is to be found in the quality of relating, of communicating, of respecting and of sharing one's fundamental humanity.

CONCLUSION

Contrary to popular distortion, counselling from a transpersonal context is not all sweetness and light, nor is it about living happily ever after. In each of us there will always be unmanifest potential which is seeking actualization. At one moment transpersonal experience can be astonishing, sometimes terrifying, as it symbolizes a reality different from our everyday one. At other times, it is beautifully simple, straightforward and creatively inspiring.

Psychosynthesis maintains that the transpersonal is evolutionary in the sense of moving us forward, being our next step in manifesting our potential. It is also revolutionary, in the sense that our identifications and attachments are challenged, and old forms have to disintegrate so that the new may emerge. At times we are called upon to surrender to the experience of uncertainty and to embrace the unknown, which inevitably increases our tolerance for paradox and ambiguity. Chaos and disintegration are often the precursors of more coherency. The transpersonal dimension has its own pathology, pitfalls and promises.

The successful outcome of transpersonal counselling may be described as an expanded sense of identity, an increased acceptance of all life experience, an integration between inner and outer worlds, a revelation of meaning and the discovery of purpose. Transpersonal experience can occur at any time in the counselling work, often spontaneously and unexpectedly. Transpersonal techniques may be used throughout the course of counselling, but are most relevant after the client has gained a degree of stability and integration. They are never a substitute for psychological work but a complement to it, which deepens and provides both an inspiring and transformative agent.

Transpersonal work is often a significant element of the final phase of counselling.

8

THE FINAL PHASE OF COUNSELLING

Counselling is an open-ended journey. There is no moment which indicates that the work is finally complete or after which one is forever guaranteed happiness and well-being. Psychosynthesis maintains that self-realization is a *process* rather than an end-result. There will always be unmanifest potential, a next step for the client in actualizing herself. Through counselling she builds her resources and is increasingly able to work creatively and responsibly with her subjective and objective process.

It is difficult to define the number of sessions in a typical course of psychosynthesis counselling as it is determined by the client's motivation, needs and stated goals. It is, however, common for the counsellor to initiate periodic reviews of the work. These serve several functions. They afford the opportunity for client and counsellor to examine their therapeutic relationship and to assess the client's progress. They also provide an occasion to consider the advisability of concluding counselling. The client herself will lead the way and define the boundaries for finishing, with the counsellor offering her feedback and evaluation when appropriate. Typically, psychosynthesis counselling occurs over a period of one to three years, initially for weekly sessions which become fortnightly. In some cases, however, the client may request a predetermined number of sessions in order to address a particular issue.

Psychosynthesis counselling is also being used in GP practices for short-term, six-session assignments in which specific problems, such as panic attacks, aggression, psychosomatic symptoms, phobias, eating disorders and depression are addressed. Psychosynthesis counsellors also practise in crisis intervention centres, such as shelters for abused women and children or intermediate homes for drug offenders and delinquent adolescents.

In determining whether the final phase of counselling has been reached, the most important question to the counsellor is whether the client's primary presenting issue(s) has (have) been adequately resolved. Has the client achieved what she wanted? The most likely time to complete counselling, or alternatively to renegotiate the commitment to continue, is when the client's stated needs have been fulfilled.

Counsellor and client will often simultaneously recognize when their current cycle of work is complete. Naturally they could continue and yet there may be a shared feeling of culmination. If the counsellor initiates it wisely, finishing in itself can be a therapeutic intervention. After a substantial period of work it may be time for the client to stand alone and be her own counsellor. Can she trust her inner resources and her capacity to respond to life as it presents itself? It may also be appropriate for the client to cease defining her identity as a person who needs counselling.

When the time is ripe and completion of their work agreed upon, counsellor and client will plan the final phase. It will include the following: issues with which the client feels incomplete and which are still to be resolved; the future direction of the client's life, final assessment of the counselling; and parting and separation from the counsellor.

INCOMPLETE ISSUES

To begin the final phase of counselling the counsellor will explore areas and issues previously addressed but which may not be fully resolved. The psyche often follows a spiral pattern of growth and with any issue that the client is confronting, there may be an increasing degree of development and differentiation. It can be likened to a spiral, each turn of which leads to greater integration. For example, one client working on self-affirmation began first by learning to harness her aggressive energies which led to a healthier capacity for self-assertion. This in turn fostered an enhanced ability to take responsibility for her life. A further turn of the spiral involved self-expression and an exploration of her life purpose and direction. What began as a psychological problem (aggression) evolved into a transpersonal experience (Self-affirmation).

The counsellor's strategy is for the client to assess her existential situation for areas warranting further focus. This would not be a time to initiate work in totally new areas but to intuit places where further refinement would be valuable. The counsellor will evoke this awareness from the client, first through dialogue and questioning. If she believes, however, that something is missed, she will challenge the client to look more deeply for it. An example of this occurred when a counsellor noticed that, although the client had learned to assert herself in her social and professional life, a blind spot remained in her relationship with family members. At home she often felt victimized and impotent. The counsellor challenged her with this observation and it became the focus of a few more sessions.

The counsellor will guide the client's reflection on previous areas of work to determine if she would regret completing counselling without having given final attention to any of them. It may be simply a question of tying up loose ends, reinforcing progress or ensuring that the client has brought the necessary changes into her everyday life. Consistency between her inner and outer world is important. Without confluence between the subjective and the objective, between the client's internal awareness and external expression, she will feel incomplete.

FUTURE DIRECTION IN THE CLIENT'S LIFE

Just as treating symptoms of disease brings relief but does not heal the whole person, finishing counselling without looking at the client's future life-direction would be limited. A person does not exist in isolation but in the context of the larger whole of society and of an intricate network of relationships. This area is worthy of attention, and if it has not yet arisen, the counsellor may initiate its discussion as an element of the client's future life-direction.

At any time the client may naturally begin to question and want to explore the nature of her values and how she chooses to relate to her world. As personal harmony increases, a spontaneous concern for integrating with society is likely to arise. This is not to say that there *should* be such concerns in the client but that it seems to be a natural tendency. This idea is congruent with Maslow's (1954) hierarchy of needs, which proposes that, as personal survival, safety and self-esteem needs are fulfilled, the individual will move towards a more universal orientation, a natural expansion of consciousness and concern for the larger whole.

In psychosynthesis terms, experience of the transpersonal Self and the superconscious reflect values that transcend egocentric concerns and affirm participation in the larger whole. Despite authenticity and freedom, individual identity is not the end-result but leads to a recognition of inter-dependence and to a more creative response to life. The individual disidentifies as a separate unit and expands her identity to include the world around her and makes life choices which are consistent with this larger identity. Inevitably this leads to an exploration of life purpose as described in Chapter 7.

Generally in the field of counselling, an often neglected factor in deter-mining behaviour is the client's perception of reality. Out of her experience of reality grows her sense of what life and its meaning is and of who she is. This is a psychological question, distinct from any issue of dogma or ideology, but is a context which may unconsciously pervade the client's experience and perception of life. The counsellor does not have a 'right reality' for her to aspire towards but rather will facilitate her explo-ration of essential questions such as: What is my place in the world? How do I live my life? How do I fit in with the larger whole?

The counsellor will help the client to define and clarify these issues as they arise, but with no imposition or assertion of her own philosophy or beliefs. She will adopt a totally non-directive stance in this exploration and merely provide the climate for the client to reflect and illumine her think-ing. The counsellor is aware that it is the client's questions to herself which are valuable, rather than any specific answer.

Feelings of responsibility for the state of society, for social issues, for global concerns are not seen to be projections of self-interest but valued as authentic responses. An individual's deep inner response to social and global conditions will greatly affect her sense of well-being. There may be pain for the whole – not neurotic personal pain – but genuine concern and a true desire for a life which both respects and is confluent with a greater good. For example, common feelings that may arise are despair and a sense of meaninglessness, fear of a lack of collective well-being, anger at the inequalities of life, guilt about one's own comfortable existence, frus-tration at a seeming inability to make a difference and sorrow for others.

In the final stage of counselling the counsellor will validate the client's questioning and awareness of her relationship to society and incorporate it in establishing her future direction. Together they will focus on what her next steps are in the major areas of her life, including how and in what way she wants to relate to the larger whole. The counsellor's strategy is for the client to complete counselling with a clear vision of and plan for her personal and professional life. This will be achieved first by experiencing subjectively what is essential and then by creating a programme of inner and outer action which honours her vision.

FINAL ASSESSMENT OF THE JOURNEY OF COUNSELLING

Over the course of counselling the client has undertaken an exploration of her inner and outer life, her problems and difficulties, her strengths and gifts, her light and darkness and the purpose of her life. Most likely she has shown courage by taking risks, exposed her vulnerability and allowed intimacy, all perhaps for the first time. An essential aspect of finishing counselling is for the counsellor and the client to define and articulate that exploration. The counsellor will encourage the client to take an overview of her journey from the onset of counselling, how she has progressed and where she has now arrived. This will focus upon the major issues that the client has worked through and how she dealt with them. Depending on the length of counselling, this assessment may take more than one session.

The purpose of such appraisal is to enable the client to affirm the progress she has made, recognize what she has achieved and reinforce her sense of competency. It also enables her to identify the inner resources she has developed and to see how they may be available to her in the future. In overview, the client's journey has been a rich one with much to be acknowledged in her capacity for regeneration and transformation. This will be achieved through dialogue and reflection, with the counsellor taking an affirmative role.

SEPARATING FROM THE COUNSELLOR

Summary of Therapeutic Relationship

Over the course of counselling the relationship between the counsellor and the client follows an evolutionary process which, although not linear, exhibits a clear progression towards autonomy and independence. The counsellor will bear this evolution in mind throughout the counselling but particularly in the final phase, as it provides her with a significant guideline to the client's situation. The evolution can be described in the following way.

The past   Initially, along with establishing a therapeutic alliance, there was an element of transference. The client does not perceive the counsellor as she truly is but her perception is coloured and conditioned by her own childhood dynamics. To varying degrees, the client's unconscious childhood patterns assert themselves. This has been discussed in detail in Chapter 5.

The present   In the first phase of counselling, depending upon the degree of the client's disturbance, the counsellor provides a point of reference. She represents that which the client cannot yet be in touch with in herself, an inclusive place which is non-judgementally aware. She offers a reminder that the client is fundamentally worthy of acceptance, that she can heal herself and find meaning in her life, and that she has the potential for self-responsibility.

In a sense the counsellor has been a symbol for the 'I' or centre of identity for the client while she finds that place in her own being – a symbol for compassion and acceptance, for clear awareness, for validation of experience and for recognition of potential. The counsellor held a vision of the client as a Self until she could experience that reality for herself. She models for the client healthier and more authentic possibilities for self-love and affirmation.

This is not to say that the counsellor is some kind of saint, but it is this function of *reminding* that is important. Temporarily the counsellor intentionally provides a coherent and unified reminder of the wholeness which the client cannot yet experience. While addressing the difficulties in her life the client gradually finds this capacity within herself. Her own centre of identity emerges organically as she becomes increasingly conscious and able to confront her life situation and make the necessary choices for change.

Person to person   Although implicit throughout, increasingly prominent is the human relationship, with the client and counsellor beginning to relate as two adults, two centres, two identities. The client becomes more and more able to perceive the counsellor as she really is, with her own human personality with strengths and vulnerabilities. She gradually ceases to be seen as the authority with all the answers, the omnipotent parent, the carrier of order and meaning. It is probable that the counsellor is showing more and more of herself to the client and the client's perception is becoming more mature and realistic.

Ideally, by the termination of counselling, client and counsellor are working together as two autonomous but interconnected beings to address the client's issues and unfoldment. The counsellor becomes a clear and conscious friend available to mirror and give feedback. They are two equals relating, exploring and making meaning of the client's life situation.

Completion of the Therapeutic Relationship

To complete the final phase of counselling, it is also essential to complete the therapeutic relationship between the counsellor and client. Through dialogue and reflection they will review the evolution of their relationship over the course of counselling and the impact it had on their work together. The counsellor will be attentive to the transference issues and how they evolved, with particular reference to any remnants of childhood patterns. As much time as is needed will be spent on expressing unspoken communication, incomplete gestalts in the relationship, acknowledgements and appreciations.

The counsellor will see this work as the final opportunity to address any remaining transference issues. She will encourage any final assertions the client might need to make. For example, one client, when finishing counselling, needed to communicate to the counsellor several moments from the past when she had felt irritated with her. Another client realized that she could not fully say goodbye to the counsellor without communicating to her deep feelings of gratefulness.

At least one session will be spent saying goodbye. At this moment, a surprising number of clients experience a reassertion of transference. A crisis will suddenly emerge, or surprising feelings of dependency and an unwillingness to let go, or separation anxiety presents itself. Saying goodbye is rarely painless for both client and counsellor. The chances are, for both, that it has been a significant relationship with multi-level engagement. The reality of finishing counselling can trigger a regressive pull against change, especially where the client is letting go of a major source of support. For other clients who feel ambivalence at having exposed so much and been so vulnerable there is also relief.

CONCLUSION

The successful outcome of psychosynthesis counselling may be described as an expanded sense of identity, in which the Self is viewed as the context of life experience. This expanded sense of identity often awakens a motivation which includes self-enhancement but one which interfaces with the larger whole. What is good for the individual integrates with what is good for the larger whole, and individual ego boundaries enlarge towards more social and global well-being. Increased tolerance for paradox and ambiguity is exhibited and inner and outer experience become more harmonious and confluent.

Although there is no way of proving increased compassion, altruistic well-being or the capacity for love, these qualities have been observed manifesting as an offshoot of transpersonal work. Once awakened to the transpersonal dimension of existence, life itself may be held in a different perspective and subsequent personal behaviour will reflect this consciousness.

Paradoxically, the experience of the transpersonal dimension is often accompanied by an increased sense of personal freedom and a fresh sense of inner direction and purpose. This healthy outcome is to a large extent ascertained by the context established by the counsellor and her skill at integrating it with the content presented by the client. The process is mutually determined in the therapeutic relationship between counsellor and client. From the perspective of psychosynthesis counselling the counsellor best serves the client by establishing a broad transpersonal context within which to work with whatever content the client presents. In this way the counsellor welcomes the client as a being who is fundamentally rich with integrity and who possesses the inner resources for optimum health and participation in life.

9

Nancy: A Case History

The Initial Interview

Nancy, an attractive and dignified woman of forty-six, sought coun-selling. She would not normally have done so, but when her closest friends who had supported her for many months tired of doing so, she reluctantly admitted that she needed professional help. Nancy had reached the end of her tether and the end of her friends' support at the same time.

An intense three-and-a-half year love affair with a married man had ended after great conflict and pain. She had been unhappy for eighteen months, mourning the loss of this relationship. She was now in a deep depression, unable to work, and at times crying uncontrollably and inap-propriately. At the initial interview she reported to the counsellor that there were millions of voices in her head rattling away at her and that she was afraid she was going mad. She felt stuck and also, while maintaining a relatively competent front, she felt in danger of losing control.

Nancy confessed, much later, that she was clutching at counselling as her last hope and had felt desperate that the counsellor would not take her on. She revealed that she had felt that she had to be an 'acceptable good girl' for the counsellor. It is useful to take note that even at the initial interview, the client may experience a fear of rejection. If the client is not appropriate for the form of counselling or particular counsellor, this must be handled sensitively.

Initial Motivation: Freedom from Pain

Being in the throes of a major life crisis, Nancy stated five initial reasons (motivations) for seeking counselling:

1 She desperately wanted the man who had left her to come back. And when he did, if he did, she wanted him to find her a calm, positive, feminine and wise woman. She did not want to be alone.
2 She wanted to stop weeping so inappropriately and stop embarrassing herself.
3 Several previous men in her life had told her that she was masculine, aggressive and controlling. She felt very unfeminine herself, except in her sexual life, for which she loathed her vulnerability. She wanted to stop being aggressive and to rediscover her lost femininity. She was also aware that her relationships with men always failed, in part because she usually chose unavailable men, and she wanted to find out why she did this.
4 Nancy had a stomach ulcer which she linked to the fact that she felt angry a lot and wanted to get rid of both the ulcer and her anger.
5 She was haunted by a recurring question, 'What am I going to do with the rest of my life?' She felt that she had never really achieved anything significant and that it was too late now. She felt doomed to a life of meaninglessness.

Establishing a Working Hypothesis

There were key pointers for the counsellor to formulate her working hypothesis of the journey Nancy might take in the course of counselling, of the sides of Nancy's personality she might help her to understand better (2 and 4) and of other factors that needed to be brought to greater awareness and developed (3).

Nancy's last hope from counselling (5) was an indication of a deeper sense of purpose than her initial motivation to salve the pain and regain her composure; the counsellor would be open for other signs of her desire to go beyond her immediate difficulties. This urge towards a state of health greater than merely mending the pain constitutes a search for purpose.

All of the above emerged through the counsellor's careful questioning about Nancy's background, and about her attitudes and feelings towards life and herself. (See p. 65 for a detailed breakdown of an initial interview.)

The counsellor also asked Nancy to write an autobiography which filled in important historical events and revealed much more about how Nancy saw herself. It also provided a kind of *taking-stock* experience for Nancy as she found herself ordering her past life on to paper, choosing which events she thought important, and seeing for herself some patterns emerging.

Nancy had many motivations for coming to counselling, which the counsellor included in her assessment and formulation of a working hypothesis. These motivating factors demanded immediate attention, and basic psychological work needed to be done to alleviate her foreground suffering. To illustrate the connection between the client's immediate motivation and emerging purpose, here is the counsellor's *working hypothesis*: Two themes seemed apparent in Nancy's presentation of her difficulties. Projection and idealization, and an underlying search for meaning. ('What am I going to do with the rest of my life?')

The counsellor surmised that Nancy had invested her core identity in every man she was involved with and experienced disproportionate grief at the loss of these relationships. Psychologically, she had identified with these men, both idealizing them and projecting on to them her own positive qualities. The counsellor knew that on one level, both were defence mechanisms unconsciously operating in Nancy to avoid facing her poor self-image. However, on another, perhaps deeper, level, the counsellor sensed that she seemed to have *given up* something of her true Self to these men.

As we will see in more detail later, the counsellor uncovered that Nancy had projected on to the love relationships in her life the aspiration and possibility to realize her creative potential. She had repressed her talents and qualities, for example her power, her initiative and her desire to express herself, in order to win the love and approval she so desperately sought from these men.

This repression became apparent through working on a recurring dream Nancy had had for several weeks, which the counsellor suggested she relive with mental imagery (see p. 54). In the dream, she was in an operating room watching as surgeons were about to cut off someone's leg. Nancy let out a scream remembering the pain of 'having something cut off'. The counsellor guided her to identify with the woman in the dream. She easily did this and discovered what had been cut off in her was 'her ambition, wanting to do something important in the world, something that was unique to her and not necessarily family expectations'.

This insight opened Nancy's eyes to an awareness that she needed to reown all of the positive aspects of herself that she had previously lost or cut off in order to have relationships which gave a false sense of security and cost too much of herself. The counsellor suggested that she explore the deeper meaning of this and what she could learn through it. Nancy found that what really mattered to her was her own creativity, her need to find her unique place in the world and to give expression to qualities inside her which were seeking expression. The counsellor remarked that not surprisingly, these qualities were exactly those that she had perceived in her male friends – power, love and intuition.

The counsellor's working hypothesis, which much later proved to be fairly accurate, was that Nancy had repressed her deeper experience of herself and her desire to create meaning in her life, by being stuck in these recurring patterns with men and had really been working out her power and creativity through them. She further surmised that Nancy would come to realize this if she reowned those projections, both the positive and the negative, as well as actively working to discover some purpose in her life. It seemed as if those two threads were coming together through the very painful experience of losing her relationship.

NANCY'S BACKGROUND

Born in London in 1939, Nancy lived in twenty-nine different places in England and America before she was eight. Her father left for the war when Nancy was six months old; her mother divorced him and remarried when Nancy was seven, at which time a half-sister was born and the nanny who brought Nancy up, and whom she both loved and feared, left.

In 1947 the family moved to Australia where Nancy lived until she was nineteen. She went to boarding school, and then at seventeen travelled to Europe with her mother by boat. They stayed in Venice where she had her first sexual experience. They went on to France where Nancy was to go to school. However, terrified she was pregnant, she told her mother (an awful experience), who consequently took her back to Australia. After discovering that she was not pregnant after all, her mother sent Nancy to secretarial college.

In 1959 Nancy went to London where she met up with her 'first real love', a man her own age whom she had met in 1956. She found work in the film business and had a live-in affair with an older, famous athlete. The following year, when she was twenty years old, Nancy went to California to meet her father. She found him to be very different than she had imagined. The picture her mother had painted of him throughout her childhood was quite different from the quiet, rather tender, soft man that she met. She stayed with him and his wife in California, during which time incestuous sexual contact occurred. She revealed this story in the fourth session and curiously said she did not really feel there was anything wrong with it, nor did she feel guilty about the incestuous contact.

After some months, she returned to Australia and at twenty-three married Bill. In 1964 her first son Alex was born, and in 1967 her second son Steven. By the end of that year her husband said he was leaving, claiming he was unfulfilled sexually in the marriage. Nancy took the boys to her parents in Malta where they lived until the end of 1969, when, under pressure from her mother, Nancy decided to divorce Bill. Nancy spent the 1970s living in England doing a variety of grotty jobs to support herself and bring up her boys. She got support from her mother, who bought her a house.

In 1980, when she was forty-one, Nancy met and fell deeply in love with Gordon, a married man. She worked for him in an advertising agency and they maintained an intense love affair. From the beginning it seemed that this relationship seemed to include and amplify so many of the repeated patterns she had had in the past with men, all the way back to her incestuous relationship with her father. With Gordon, she talked about the overwhelming sexual relationship and how she felt she had very little choice. This was a theme throughout her life, including several incidents during therapy; that if she became attracted to a man at all she would not be able to say no. She also spoke of a 'special essence' that they seemed to share which was equally overwhelming. She elaborated that they shared a special feeling of unity and brought out the best in each other. It was in 1984 that he cut off the relationship abruptly and Nancy did not see him again.

THE INITIAL PHASE OF COUNSELLING

Subpersonalities

Nancy's opening statement in the first session had expressed a fear of going mad. She felt overwhelmed by many frantic voices in her head. They came tumbling out as she described her inner chaos, fear and inability to think clearly. Her uncontrollable crying indicated deep distress. Evoking further motivation at that moment was inappropriate and the counsellor responded to Nancy's immediate experience.

She asked Nancy if there was any one voice speaking louder and over-riding the others. Nancy easily slipped into a stern voice, which was judging her vehemently and telling her how pathetic and hopeless she was. This harsh critic told her that she would never be good enough to be loved and that the broken relationship was all that she deserved.

The counsellor asked Nancy how she felt towards this unyielding judge, at which Nancy burst into tears and, with the counsellor's encouragement, cried throughout the entire session. Clearly she believed that the critic spoke the truth. In addition to staying compassionately present, the counsellor helped Nancy to clarify and define the predominant voices she was experiencing. The first session concluded with the counsellor using the educative function to tell Nancy the principle of subpersonalities; the experience that each person may have many different parts inside, which are sometimes in conflict. With this knowledge Nancy was immediately relieved and was able to see that although confused and distressed, she was not crazy.

For several sessions, the counsellor worked mainly with Nancy's imme-diate presenting issues, establishing trust between the two of them and using gestalt dialogue to help Nancy separate and identify those voices 'yapping away at her' (see p. 86 for a description of subpersonality work). Nancy found this increase in her awareness, and the new sense of clarity, very relieving, and by the third session she was able to focus on the pres-ent moment, rather than fly uncontrollably off into the past and future.

Chronic Life Patterns

From the beginning the counsellor saw a chronic life pattern emerge as Nancy told her about the sexual experiences with her father and the con-sistent overtures he had made to her (at twenty years old when she saw him for the first time since she was five), and of feeling betrayed by him. Nancy's parents had divorced in her early childhood. She said, 'during my childhood I built up a fantasy that he was a perfect and glamorous man (working in the sports world) and he would be the one man who would love and understand me for what I was.'

In the following session the counsellor asked Nancy to go back to the time when she re-met her father: with eyes closed Nancy was asked to see it all again, as if watching a film (see p. 54 for mental imagery), with the counsellor stopping her at significant 'frames' and asking about her feel-ings and responses throughout the experience. Nancy claimed to feel no guilt, but when the counsellor asked what decision she had made about men, about loving and being loved, she said, 'All men are alike. You have to have sex with them to get them to notice/love you. They lie.' The counsellor further asked Nancy what she needed to say to her father that she hadn't then. Nancy cried repeatedly, 'Leave me alone!' It emerged that a year after Nancy had left her father in America, her father, who was only in his fifties, had died of a heart attack. He had written her love letters which she hadn't answered. The guilt that she was in some sense responsible for her father's death remained with her.

The following are the counsellor's analyses of Nancy's basic psychological state. She saw that the complex encounter with Nancy's father contributed to her belief system about men, and her basic pattern in relationships as well as her self-image. Nancy had told her that when as a child she did something that her mother didn't like, she would shout, 'You're just like your father!' – meaning irresponsible, volatile, emotional. Nancy's stepfather was a cool, detached man who likewise had disallowed her feelings, calling her over-emotional when she asserted herself in discussions, demanding that she be logical if he was to engage with her. There was no natural bonding and rebellion process for Nancy during her childhood, no chance for her to love and yet negotiate her own boundaries; this was compounded by the sexual experiences with her real father.

Nancy had learned from these early dynamics that her power and assertion were *bad* and that expression of strong emotion was *bad*. She grew to see herself as over-emotional, therefore unlovable, and came to believe that if she said 'no' to men then they would leave (in her father's case by dying). Both her natural assertiveness and her loving side became distorted, the one into a capable bossiness, the other into a controlling caring for men combined with an anxious belief that she was responsible for making them happy. Indeed, part of Nancy's initial motivation for coming into counselling was to *get rid of* her assertive side.

At this stage the counsellor kept these analyses to herself, but during the following few sessions Nancy's awareness of these introverted messages grew. The counsellor aimed for Nancy, instead of again suppressing her assertiveness or emotional nature, to get in touch with and, perhaps for the first time, begin to express through cathartic work (see p. 51) her anger and resentment at not being accepted. Much later, through dialogue, the counsellor helped Nancy to clarify the paralysing effect of being denied this fundamental human right. She became aware of her anger towards her father and towards men in general, feeling that she had needed to be loved as a little girl just for who she was; not because of her body or what she was willing to give. The sexual contact with her father had 'cut off that awareness'.

She connected this insight with other relationships in her family: she said:

> My experience of family is of a collection of individuals with no purpose, all arguing and playing their expected roles. My own role, as *black sheep*, the one who embarrasses the rest by being different, with a different outlook on life and holding different socially unacceptable values, was a very stuck atrophied role, impossible to step out of. The family pressure for me to stay in that role always leaves me with feelings of anger, frustration and then passive silence.

Third-chair technique   In one session the counsellor asked Nancy to move into the 'third chair' during a gestalt dialogue, in order to ascertain whether she was able to disidentify from the angry struggle that she was playing out, in this case between Gordon and herself (see p. 99 for disiden-tification). Instead, Nancy's critic subpersonality re-emerged, and the counsellor helped her to connect this critical voice inside with her mother. In the role of this critic/mother subpersonality, she commented: 'I can't allow Nancy to love or be loved, something I never had. My life would be meaningless, she would have won.'

While startled to discover this intense competitiveness between herself and her mother, Nancy said she was quite unable to let it go. The counsellor challenged her to recognize how identified she was with the battle between herself and her mother, and how this battle was limiting her psychological freedom. Nonetheless over the following weeks Nancy had several meetings with her mother that were quite different in quality.

As a grounding technique (see p. 62) the counsellor suggested that Nancy might risk communicating more deeply with her mother. So for the first time Nancy asked her mother about the divorce from her father. Nancy's mother confessed that as a child, she herself had been sexually interfered with and she'd never told anyone in her entire life. To her surprise Nancy saw the frail, vulnerable side of her mother, and, while their relationship remained difficult, some real communication began to open up for them. The counsellor's guiding her to express her anger to her mother in the safety of the therapeutic session had freed up the psychological space for Nancy to see and respond to her mother in a fresh way.

More work with Nancy's chronic life pattern   Nancy saw herself as 'addicted' to sexual/emotional relationships, as someone with no choice. In the sixth session the counsellor and Nancy worked with mental imagery on a consistent feeling with which she was stuck and in conflict. She felt desperate to go back to Gordon, but also wanted to run away and hide (not be seen). Nancy's statement was, 'If I don't go back, I'll never see him again.' At this point an intervention from the counsellor helped Nancy to see the parallels with her relationship with her father.

Nancy saw further parallels between her relationship with her father and Gordon. Gordon and her father shared the same name, they were both athletes, as was her first husband, and many times when she was talking about her memories of the contact she had had with her father she likened it to Gordon. She felt in some ways responsible for Gordon, Gordon's welfare, unhappily married Gordon, unhappily married father. She felt somehow that it was her responsibility to take care of them, to inspire them, to get them to be happy.

And so the process was deepened, as the counsellor guided Nancy back to an earlier stage in her life. She asked Nancy if she could choose to walk away, free of the hold her father had on her. She could not, until the counsellor asked her to get an image for this feeling of no choice (so taking the process yet deeper). Nancy saw herself as a little girl shunted around unwillingly from school to school, always losing her friends. With the counsellor's prompting she was able to recognize the small vulnerable child in her, and as an adult, Nancy was able to take the child by the hand, in mental imagery, and walk away. With this new connection to the child subpersonality within her, she now had the possibility of choosing, as an adult, to do something different in relation to Gordon, her lost love.

More sessions were spent grounding Nancy's new-found contact with this child subpersonality. They explored more memories from that time, expanding on Nancy's feelings for her child. The counsellor encouraged her to relate to that child within her, for whom she felt increasing compassion. Through gestalt dialogue (see p. 97) Nancy gradually got to know her, and was able to assess and meet the child's psychological needs for security and love. The counsellor stressed in this work how Nancy had the potential to meet these needs from the *inside*, rather than being dependent on *outside* validation (in Nancy's case through relationships with men).

THE MIDDLE PHASE OF COUNSELLING

Soon Nancy reported experiencing herself 'free of her addiction to her past relationship'. She was consciously experiencing the ability to choose in her life, particularly with regard to men. Indeed, she was amazed on several occasions to notice that men were interested in her, but that she could step back and choose whether or not she wanted sexual contact. At this opportune moment the counsellor initiated the Self-identification exercise, during which Nancy had an experience of a new identity which was beyond her old self-image with men. She felt immensely liberated.

In one session the counsellor introduced the idea of the positive qualities deeply underlying events, patterns and relationships. She encouraged Nancy to write about previous relationships, again particularly with men, and to look especially for the quality she had been in touch with in the man (for example, strength), the one evoked in her (for example, joy) and the one that summed up the essence of the relationship (for example, intensity). The counsellor's purpose here was to encourage Nancy to move deeper than the level of working only with the content of her chronic pattern, to become aware of the underlying and/or larger dynamic. The counsellor suggested the use of the technique of evoking and developing a desired quality (see p. 137) which brought a transpersonal component into their work. Nancy found that this opened her eyes to potentials in herself which she had not dared to dream of having, and her sense of self-worth dramatically increased.

In several subsequent sessions they also looked at these relationships from the perspective of *behaviour and needs*: again distinguishing the surface level of behaviour (for example, intense sexuality), from the deeper one of what Nancy *wanted* (for example, to feel loved), moving finally to the yet deeper level of what Nancy sensed she really *needed* from the relationship (for example, nourishment/acceptance/security). The counsellor used basic subpersonality work, gestalt dialogue and mental imagery to achieve this; transpersonal work with 'the wise being' enabled Nancy to discover the deepest level of her need.

Working on Problems from Two Dimensions

With the presenting problem now relatively stabilized, Nancy's yearning for some meaning in her life began to emerge. She would often say in these latter sessions, 'If Gordon doesn't come back to me, what am I going to do with the rest of my life?' The counsellor developed a hypothesis that Nancy had suppressed her own creativity and power through being stuck in these repeated sexual patterns with men, and had been working out her creativity and power *through them*.

So the first step would be for Nancy to reown these projections, a prerequisite for finding some purpose in life, and exploring a meaningful career. The counsellor focused Nancy on the quality of a man or relationship, rather than content, which helped her to consider reowning the same qualities in herself.

As synchronicity would have it, a number of former lovers turned up out of the blue, so Nancy was given the opportunity to complete with them *actually*, while she could look at the relationship during therapy more *theoretically*. A further real-life event at this time helped her to see her pattern of rescuing unhappily married men very clearly: during a holiday the husband of a friend made sexual advances to her, and Nancy was able to say 'no'. Through dialogue with the counsellor she saw how she had automatically cast the wife in the role of baddy, the husband as the victim and herself as rescuer, *responsible* for the 'hero's' happiness: an endless recapitulation of the chronic pattern established with her father. All this suddenly became blindingly clear, at the same time losing its charge; she was able to choose to say 'no', without fear of loss, rejection or diminishment. At a chance meeting with Gordon she realized she didn't want him any more and that she felt complete with him, and without him!

A key element in Nancy's search for purpose was her relationship with her own power towards which she felt, at best, ambivalent. For the most part she rejected it, in the belief that 'men didn't like powerful women as it was unfeminine'. Once again the counsellor addressed Nancy's unconscious rather than looking at this belief with the rational mind: she asked Nancy to get an image for the part of her that could express and exert power. Nancy came up with Queen Boudicca, whom she at first rejected.

In the following session Nancy announced that she wanted to make Queen Boudicca more attractive and more feminine. The counsellor queried what this actually meant to her. In Nancy's eyes this meant evoking the vulnerable part of the Queen, the part that needed love. They did this, but following her earlier hypothesis the counsellor also asked Nancy to write about power, about what it was like to assert herself, what happened when she did, how she felt and so on. The counsellor followed up on this exercise in the next session and discussing it led to Nancy having an important realization *vis-à-vis* her relationship with her lost lover and indeed other men: that, contrary to her beliefs up till then, it was not her powerful assertive side she considered so feminine, it was this desperate need for love and approval that stopped her seeing what was really happening in her relationships.

The counsellor spent several sessions helping Nancy to ground (see

p. 62) her realizations about relationships and herself. The counsellor encouraged her, through experiential work, to look at fantasy versus reality, what was *really* happening as opposed to what she *imagined* was going on. During this work a new sophistication in Nancy's ability to use the counselling started to emerge. The imagery she presented became more abstract and transpersonal, images of light and nothingness, an existential quality and sense of universality; an ability to step back from her feelings and disidentify also became evident. Nancy's ability to disidentify from the emotions that swept through her, to see that she, her 'I', was something more than her thoughts, fears, feelings and so on, prompted the counsellor to encourage a deeper contact in Nancy with her 'I', through again using the Self-identification exercise.

The counsellor then asked Nancy, progressively to get an image for how she thought others saw her, for how she would like to be seen, and finally, for *who you really are*. Nancy was dismayed to produce an image of the Buddha, whose qualities were wisdom and peace. She strenuously pushed it away, claiming that she disliked all religion and that the image looked remote and cold. Still very much identified with herself as a warm, feeling person, this Buddha seemed inimitable to her, a betrayal of the person she thought she was. However, the image recurred many times over the subsequent course of counselling, becoming a symbol of her wise being (see p. 136), and eventually Nancy was able to accept that there was a central core to her that was wise and peaceful.

Transference

A brief incident at this time highlighted issues of transference and choice. Nancy had often referred to herself as a 'black knicker lady' (i.e. sexual), as opposed to a 'white knicker lady' ('the kind men marry'). However, the counsellor noticed that now, with her new sense of exploring her purpose, Nancy rejected this sexy persona, seeing her as bad, and the 'programme of reform' she had set for herself as good. Progress had become a 'should'. The counsellor observed a positive transference and a desire to please her which she felt was tied up with Nancy's substantial progress.

Invited to a party where she knew she would meet two attractive married men, Nancy announced how pleased she was that she knew how to say 'no', now having reformed herself. To Nancy's astonishment the counsellor asked whether or not she had a *choice* to be a 'black knicker lady' at this party. The counsellor framed the issue as being one of inner freedom, rather than following the dictates of the reformer's 'shoulds'. This turned out to be a liberating moment for Nancy as she moved from the strict, brittle world of shoulds to the demanding but satisfying approach of exercising inner choice.

The counsellor also seized the opportunity this experience provided to address the issue of transference. She challenged Nancy's 'pleasing approach' towards her and questioned whether Nancy was still free to reveal her darker aspects (like the 'black knicker lady'). She asked Nancy to talk about the 'black knicker lady' and to notice her internal responses as she did so. As she had always viewed herself as a bit of a rebel, Nancy discovered to her horror that inside, beneath the surface, there was a running commentary of: 'Be careful, make sure you are safe here, don't let your counsellor down, she has helped you so much and now you are well. You must not get it wrong again.'

Gently probing, the counsellor helped Nancy to accept this underneath voice and together they discussed how she had come to idealize her and deeply to desire her approval. Nancy acknowledged that the counsellor had become the wonderful mother that she had never had. With the transference acknowledged, they agreed to monitor Nancy's communications for honest disclosure. The counsellor often pointed out to Nancy the moments when she felt the 'good girl' operating, always with the opportunity to change the level on which she was sharing.

Longing and Resistance

When the counsellor asked Nancy what the common thing was that she wanted from all her relationships, she replied 'connectedness and containment'. The counsellor saw this response signalling a transpersonal shift in Nancy's consciousness, a moving to a larger dimension. Rather than look at particular relationships or at the past, the counsellor now helped Nancy explore how she manifested and evoked these qualities in her life, by doing ideal-model work (see p. 138).

Having identified the essential qualities that Nancy wanted from relationships, the counsellor suggested that they could now bring the abstract back into the 'concrete'. She initiated mental-imagery work with Nancy, followed by rational interpretation, by asking her to envisage, with as much detail as possible, an 'ideal' relationship. The ideal-model exercise, an immensely powerful tool when used at the right time, helped Nancy to clarify what she *did* want from a relationship, rather than continuing to dwell on what *didn't* work. In this way the counsellor helped Nancy begin to build a positive energy for change.

The tremendous steps forward that Nancy had taken and the positive and strongly transpersonal tenor now in her work precipitated a predictable backlash. (See pp. 145–8 for resistance to the transpersonal and the crisis of duality.) Several sessions were spent dealing with Nancy's sudden surge of hopelessness, feelings that she was getting nowhere and that the therapy was not working. The counsellor maintained a strongly supportive but essentially passive and unruffled presence. She knew that Nancy was unconsciously experimenting with being a 'bad' client – untogether, unpleasant, recalcitrant and depressed. She also knew that it was crucial for Nancy to be able to do this and let go of 'end-gaining' in the counselling, of the urge to be 'better' and at last get it 'right' with her mother/stepfather/counsellor.

This dark night gave way to a clearer and more realistic dawn, which the counsellor had expected, provided Nancy was able to stay with her temporary backlash. The pace of the work had slowed and the excitement of sudden realizations and resolutions gave way to a period of thoughtful, solid work. The counsellor focused Nancy on dialoguing about her belief systems and used gestalt identification and dialogue to work on her primary relationship with her mother, interspersed with detailed subpersonality work. While much of the content of the work might have seemed similar to the themes of earlier sessions, Nancy had clearly moved to another turn of the spiral. The counsellor affirmed the new quality which was evident in both the work and in Nancy. It was as if she had matured over the last five weeks and she appeared more centred, more accepting of herself and less volatile.

The counsellor used this appropriate moment to invite Nancy to explore her relationships with her two sons, which were problematic and often difficult. Through dialogue, the counsellor helped Nancy to discover how each son was 'playing out' two sides of herself, the one her energetic, organized, ambitious side; the other her lazy, unmotivated, life-denying side. The counsellor perceived that Nancy's identity was now strong enough for her to admit and explore this latter aspect of herself, this existential blackness (as opposed to received and introjected negative opinion). Using gestalt dialogue the counsellor helped her to deal with this 'poisonous' part of herself, which she wanted to cut out, and the aspiring, idealistic part of herself, which had been so badly thwarted in her teens.

The counsellor encouraged Nancy to experience fully the deep well of her sadness, her regret and especially the negative, pessimistic part of herself – all feelings that had hitherto lain well buried beneath the more flamboyant emotions and the business that she habitually expressed. In this quiet and sombre experience, the counsellor supported Nancy to be fully in touch with the awesome experience of stripping away the noise and the activity to face a primal and existential truth about herself. The counsellor surmised that deep down Nancy was afraid to let go of her struggle to be different and potentially to collapse. The counsellor suggested that she, there and then, 'let go into being herself', which provoked deep cathartic sobbing and led on, in subsequent sessions, to the issue of authenticity, and the start of Nancy's drive to be fully *herself*, with all the different aspects of her personality, to embrace the fearsome and negative along with the positive.

THE FINAL PHASE OF COUNSELLING

Incomplete Issues

Shortly afterwards, in another key session, the power–neediness struggle reasserted itself, in the shape of two vivid subpersonalities, the Amazon and the needy child (another aspect of the role played out by Nancy's younger son in his refusal to grow up and embrace life).

Nancy was now working for a large international charity putting her organizational and assertive skills to good and satisfying use. Just as she had once rejected her powerful side she now could not accept the neediness in herself. She said, 'I must maintain dignity – the idea of letting go terrifies me – if I am needy, I lose all control.' The counsellor pointed out to Nancy that the autonomous Amazon refused to comfort this most fragile part of herself, refused to give her the warmth and acceptance that Nancy herself had lacked as a child. This reminded Nancy of how her choice in men echoed her own uncaring and critical attitude to her needy child.

At this point the counsellor initiated gestalt dialogue between these two parts and Nancy was able finally to allow herself to experience the gratification of comforting and being comforted. The counsellor aimed for her to perceive the distortion in her image of the needy child: as weak and feeble rather than open and soft, as over-demanding rather than deserving of love and care.

Following on from the previous work, the counsellor anticipated another turn of the spiral of Nancy's increasing acceptance of herself. Nancy presented some spontaneous images which were very primal – the deep sea, a harbour, a terrifying huge 'force' under the water. The counsellor asked Nancy to identify with the force. She said, 'I am huge, threatening, I don't want to be seen; I surge to indicate that I'm here, but stay below the surface. I groan, people are terrified.' The counsellor asked Nancy, as the force, what she needed, and her reply was to break out. Unexpectedly the force announced, 'I am Love', as it broke the surface in bright, diffused light. This was an immensely cathartic moment for Nancy, which the counsellor reinforced, and the rest of the session was spent quietly being with her feelings and her understanding both of the power of her love and how much it had been suppressed.

In subsequent sessions the counsellor helped Nancy to ground these new insights. Through dialogue and bringing the mind to bear, the counsellor helped Nancy quietly to talk through this overwhelming experience. Nancy understood how her fear led her to seek acceptance and inclusion before asserting herself, both with men and in relation to her mother and family. The counsellor helped her to refine this understanding by discussing the difference between acceptance and resignation. She then initiated an exploration of how Nancy might use her learnings about her love in her current relationships.

Future Direction in the Client's Life

Exploring the future direction of her life required another turn of the spiral in Nancy's relationship to men. She had a new relationship, which the counsellor pointed out to her was showing signs of taking a different course to previous ones. The counsellor guided her to readdress once more her feelings towards her father with the intention of undoing the retroflection of feeling guilty and blaming herself for his death. By using gestalt dialogue, the counsellor helped Nancy to experience at last that she had not failed her father – but that he had failed her through his sexual violations.

In order to rebuild a positive potential for Nancy in her relationships with men, the counsellor suggested that they use mental imagery to envisage her meeting men as equals. With the counsellor's support Nancy was able wholeheartedly to accept her new relationship. She pointed out to Nancy that having experienced trust and respect in their relationship had enabled Nancy to take risks, to do things differently and to overturn her habitual defensive responses. Nancy saw that a similar possibility existed for her in other relationships in future.

Additionally, the counsellor suggested a few sessions of exploring Nancy's life purpose, first subjectively with transpersonal techniques and later objectively translating her experience of purpose into action. This work unfolded beautifully as Nancy's work in the international charity was already fulfilling her value system, and she made a deeper commitment to it. She decided to seek a new position within the organization which would allow her to express more of her 'force' of love.

The counselling was now drawing to a close. In one of the last few sessions the counsellor brought up Queen Boudicca again and asked Nancy how she felt about this symbol for female power, now that she had found the connectedness and containment she had sought in a relationship and also had a career that was focusing her sense of purpose in the world. Nancy reflected and found she responded to an earthy quality she now detected in Boudicca, as opposed, she said, to the calm, detached, slightly ethereal nature of her symbol for masculine wisdom, the Buddha.

The counsellor guided her to work with these two polarities and suggested that Nancy identify first with one and then the other; and then moving swiftly, literally stepping from one to the other, they came to a point of integration, a 'feminine, powerful wisdom' that Nancy dubbed the 'wisdom of the courtesan'. The courtesan represented for her a synthesis of the masculine and the feminine, of love and will, of assertion and inclusion. The counsellor concluded this work by discussing with Nancy what life would be like for her if she could fully express this feminine, powerful wisdom, this integration of male and female qualities.

Final Assessment of the Journey of Counselling

It was a question which, in a sense, could only be answered by Nancy living her life, but the theme of integration, of both/and rather than either/or, was prominent during the final sessions as the counsellor and Nancy went over some of the experiences, themes and learnings of their work together: letting go of struggle/being terrified of letting go; being powerful and needy and still being loved; protecting herself and also understanding and caring for her own frailty; being open and maintaining her point of view; her rich resources and subpersonalities, Boudicca and Buddha, black knicker lady and courtesan, the inner child and the adult Nancy.

Separating from the Counsellor

During this process of ending the counsellor made a point of acknowledging her own feelings for Nancy, her affection for her and respect for the courage she had shown on their journey together. She acknowledged that it had sometimes been arduous, confusing or frustrating. She emphasized what Nancy had achieved, how far she had come in finding answers for her initial questions and alternatives for patterns that had been blocking her life. The counsellor also gave Nancy suggestions for the focus of future work on herself, whether within counselling or simply on her own, with the considerable skills and resources she had acquired.

Nancy also had much to say to the counsellor both in terms of things she had felt but not previously said and to express her gratitude. She herself was able to trace their relationship through stages similar to childhood, from dependency to autonomy; from fear to confrontation; from parent–child to person to person. Most important to Nancy had been the counsellor's *bifocal* vision of her – the relief of being seen as fundamentally all right and worthy of love, and yet still to have her pain and problems be embraced. She valued highly the way in which her perception and experience of herself had so tremendously expanded and appreciated the trust the counsellor had for her.

It was on this *note*, after two and half years and some sixty sessions, that the counsellor and Nancy parted.

APPENDIX

BASIC SELF-IDENTIFICATION I

This exercise has the purpose of achieving consciousness of the Self, as well as promoting the ability to focus attention sequentially on the main personality aspects, feelings, thoughts and sensations. In the form which follows, the first phase of the exercise, *disidentification*, consists of three parts. It deals with the physical, emotional and mental levels of awareness. Disidentification leads to the Self-identification phase, the recognition of oneself as a pure centre of awareness and Being.

Sit in a comfortable position, taking a few deep breaths. Make the following affirmation slowly and thoughtfully:

1   I *have* a body and I am more than my body. My body may find itself in different conditions of health and sickness, it may be rested or tired, but it is not my *self*, my real 'I'. I value my body, it is precious, and it is necessary if I am to experience and to act in the outer world. I treat it well, I keep it in good health, but it is not my true self. I *have* a body and I am more than my body.

2   I *have* emotions and I am more than my emotions. My emotions are constantly changing, sometimes in harmony, sometimes contradictorily. They may swing from love to hostility, from calm to anger, from joy to sorrow, and yet my *essence*, my true nature, does not change. 'I'

remain. Though a wave of a particular emotion may temporarily submerge me, I know that it will pass in time. Therefore I am not that emotion or any other temporary feeling. Since I can observe and understand my emotions, and then gradually learn to direct, utilize and integrate them, it is clear that they are not *myself*. I *have* emotions and I am more than my emotions.

3   I *have* a mind and I am more than my mind. My mind is a valuable tool of discovery and expression, but it is not the *essence* of my Being. Its contents are constantly changing as it grasps new ideas, knowledge and experience. Sometimes my mind is clear and sometimes cloudy. Sometimes it refuses to obey me. Therefore it cannot be *me*, my *self*. I *have* a mind and I am more than my mind.

4   What am I then? What remains after having disidentified from my body, my feelings and my mind? It is the *essence* of myself, a centre of pure consciousness. It is the permanent factor in the ever-changing flow of my personal life. It is that which gives me a sense of being, of permanence of inner balance. I affirm my identity with this centre and realize its permanency and its energy. I am a centre of being and of will, capable of observing, directing and using all my mental, emotional and physical processes. *I am I.*

BASIC SELF-IDENTIFICATION II

This exercise is an adaptation of Basic Self-Identification I and uses a different language and tone.

Sit in a comfortable position, taking a few deep breaths. Follow the instructions slowly and thoughtfully. Become aware of your body right now. Notice how your body is feeling. Notice what sensations pass through it right now. Be aware of how your body was different when you were younger, a different size and shape than it has now. You had different bodily experiences and they will change again as you grow older. Your body keeps changing from day to day; sometimes it is energetic and alert, sometimes tired and frail.

As you are aware of your body, ask yourself *who is aware?* Who is aware of this body that is constantly changing? *Who* has a body?

Now focus your attention on your feelings. Become aware of what you are feeling right now. Your feelings too are in a constant process of change. One moment they are joyful, then sad, then angry. They can move from joy to sadness, from love to hostility.

As you are aware of your feelings, ask yourself *who is aware? Who* has feelings?

Finally become aware of your thoughts. With the same impartial attitude sit back and watch your thoughts pass through your mind. What are you thinking right now? Your mind too is generally in a constant state of change. Your thoughts are sometimes clear and direct, sometimes chaotic and confused. When you were young you believed many things that you don't believe now. In the future this will again happen. Your thoughts, attitudes and belief systems are constantly changing.

In the light of this ask yourself *who is aware? Who* has a mind?

Experience yourself as a point of consciousness beyond your body, your feelings and your mind. A centre of awareness and will. Recognize yourself as a Being who has the richness of bodily sensation, emotions and thoughts. Think about the one in you who remains the same. Who you are is greater and beyond your personality.

Affirm your sense of pure beingness, of being a Self, a centre of 'I'-ness. Allow yourself to experience fully that 'I'. Experience your Being.

REFERENCES

Alberti, A. (1975) *The Will in Psychotherapy*. New York: Psychosynthesis Research Foundation.

Angyal, Andras (1965) *A Holistic Theory, Neurosis and Treatment*. New York: Viking Press.

Assagioli, Roberto (1965) *Psychosynthesis. A Manual of Principles and Techniques*. Wellingborough: Thorsons.

Assagioli, Roberto (1967) *Jung and Psychosynthesis*. New York: Psychosynthesis Research Foundation.

Assagioli, Roberto (1973) 'Roberto Assagioli: the rebirth of the soul', *New York Intellectual Digest,* August.

Assagioli, Roberto (1975) *The Resolution of Conflicts.* New York: Psychosynthesis Research Foundation.

Assagioli, Roberto (1976) *Transpersonal Inspiration and Psychological Mountain Climbing.* New York: Psychosynthesis Research Foundation.

Brown, Molly (1983) *The Unfolding Self: Psychosynthesis and Counseling.* Los Angeles: Psychosynthesis Press.

Buber, Martin (1970) *I and Thou.* New York: Scribners.

Buber, Martin (1971) *Between Man and Man.* New York: Macmillan.

Carter, Betsy (1978) 'Identity and personal freedom', *Synthesis Journal* (California Synthesis Press), II.

Clarkson, P. (1999) *Gestalt Counselling in Action.* 2nd edn. London: Sage Publications.

Crampton, Martha (1969) *The Use of Mental Imagery in Psychosynthesis*. New York: Psychosynthesis Research Foundation.

Crampton, Martha (1977) *Psychosynthesis, Some Key Aspects of Theory and Practice*. Montreal: Canadian Institute of Psychosynthesis.

Desoille, Robert (1965) *The Directed Daydream*. New York: Psychosynthesis Research Foundation issue no. 18.

Ferrucci, Piero (1982) *What We May Be*. Wellingborough: Thorsons.

Ferrucci, Piero (1990) *Inevitable Grace*. Wellingborough: Thorsons.

Firman, John and Gila, Ann (1997) *The Primal Wound: A Transpersonal View of Trauma, Addiction and Growth*. New York: State University of New York Press.

Frankl, Viktor (1970) *Man's Search for Meaning*. New York: Washington Square Press.

Frankl, Viktor (1973) *The Doctor and the Soul*. New York: Random House, Vintage Books.

Freud, Sigmund (1936) *New Introductory Lectures*. London: Pelican Books.

Freud, Sigmund (1943) *A General Introduction to Psychoanalysis*. Garden City Publishing.

Fromm, Eric (1941) *Escape from Freedom*. New York: Rhinehart.

Gordon-Brown, I. and Somers, B. (1988) 'Transpersonal psychotherapy', in J. Rowan and W. Dryden (eds), *Innovative Therapy in Britain*. Milton Keynes: Open University Press.

Grof, Stanislav (1979) *Realms of the Human Unconscious*. London: Souvenir Press (E and A Limited).

Haronian, Frank (1972) *The Repression of the Sublime*. New York: Psychosynthesis Research Foundation.

Harris, Thomas (1973) *I'm OK, You're OK*. London: Pan Books.

Hillman, James (1996) *The Soul's Code: In Search of Character and Calling*. New York: Warner Books.

Insel, P. and Jacobson, L. (1975) *What Do You Expect?* California: Cummings.

Jacobs, M. (1999) *Psychodynamic Counselling in Action*. 2nd edn. London: Sage Publications.

Jung, Carl Gustav (1933) *Modern Man in Search of a Soul*. New York: Harcourt Brace.

Jung, Carl Gustav (1954a) *The Psychology of Transference*. Princeton: Princeton University Press.

Jung, Carl Gustav (1954b) *Volume 16: The Practice of Psychotherapy*. London: Routledge and Kegan Paul.

Kaufman, Y. (1984) 'Analytical psychotherapy', in R. Corsini (ed.), *Current Psychotherapies*. Chicago, Illinois: F.E. Peacock Publishing.

Mahler, M., Pine, F. and Bergman, A. (1991) *The Psychological Birth of the Human Infant*. London: Karnac Books.

Maslow, Abraham (1954) *Motivation and Personality*. New York: Harper and Row.

Maslow, Abraham (1967) 'Self actualisation and beyond', in J.F.T. Bugental (ed.), *Challenges of Humanistic Psychology*. New York: McGraw-Hill.

Maslow, Abraham (1968) *Toward a Psychology of Being*. Wokingham: Van Nostrand Reinhold Company.

Maslow, Abraham (1971) *The Farther Reaches of Human Nature*. New York: Viking Press.

Perls, F. (1970) 'Four lectures', in J. Fagen and I. Shepherd (eds), *Gestalt Therapy Now*. New York: Harper and Row.

Progoff, Ira (1975) *At a Journal Workshop*. New York: Dialogue House Library.

Rogers, Carl R. (1961) *On Becoming a Person*. Boston: Houghton Mifflin.

Singer, June (1973) *Boundaries of the Soul*. New York: Anchor.

Vargiu, J. (1974) *Synthesis Journal Volume 7*. San Francisco, CA: Synthesis Press.

Vaughan, F. (1985) *Inward Arc*. Boston and London: New Science Library, Shambala.

Vaughan-Clark, F. (1977) 'Transpersonal perspectives in psychotherapy', *Journal of Humanistic Psychology,* Spring.

Watzlawick, Paul (1974) *Changes*. New York: Norton and Co.

Wilber, Ken (1980) *The Atman Project*. London: Theosophical Publishing House.

Wilber, Ken (1983) *Up from Eden*. London: Routledge and Kegan Paul.

Winnicott, D.W. (1987) *The Maturational Processes and the Facilitating Environment*. London: The Hogarth Press and the Institute of Psychoanalysis.

FURTHER READING

Assagioli, Roberto (1965) *Psychosynthesis: A Manual of Principles and Techniques*. Wellingborough: Thorsons.

Assagioli, Roberto (1974) *The Act of Will*. Wellingborough: Thorsons.

Assagioli, Roberto (1991) *Transpersonal Development*. Wellingborough: Thorsons.

Brown, Molly (1983) *The Unfolding Self: Psychosynthesis and Counseling*. Los Angeles: Psychosynthesis Press.

Brown, Molly (1993) *Growing Whole: Exploring the Wilderness Within*. San Francisco: Hazelden/Harper Collins.

Eastcott, Michal (1969) *The Silent Path*. London: Rider.

Ferrucci, Piero (1982) *What We May Be: The Visions and Techniques of Psychosynthesis*. Wellingborough: Thorsons.

Firman, John and Gila, Ann (1997) *The Primal Wound: A Transpersonal View of Trauma, Addiction and Growth*. New York: State University of New York Press.

Hardy, Jean (1996) *Psychology with a Soul: Psychosynthesis in Evolutionary Context*. London: Woodgrange Press.

Parfitt, Will (1990) *The Elements of Psychosynthesis*. Dorset: Element Books.

Whitmore, Diana (1986) A *Guide to the Joy of Learning: Psychosynthesis in Education*. Wellingborough: Thorsons.

INDEX